Sustaining Shared Thinking

Supporting thinking skills in young learners

Written by
Jenni Clarke
with additional material by Sally Featherstone

Published 2009 by A & C Black Publishers Limited
36 Soho Square, London W1D 3QY
www.acblack.com

First published 2007 by Featherstone Education Limited

ISBN 978-1-9050-1989-2

Text © Jenni Clarke 2007
Cover design by Kerry Ingham

The Key Issues series is edited by Sally Featherstone

A CIP record for this publication is available from the British Library.

Printed in Malta by Gutenberg Press Ltd.

This book is produced using paper that is made from wood grown in
managed, sustainable forests. It is natural, renewable and recyclable.
The logging and manufacturing processes conform to the environmental
regulations of the country of origin.

To see our full range of titles
visit **www.acblack.com**

CONTENTS

Part 1

Part 2

Introduction

Education is not just learning knowledge and skills, but the development of children's learning capacity. Education is the development of thinking clearly and creatively, implementing their own plans and communicating their ideas to others in a variety of ways.

Sue Palmer and Galina Dolya (2004)

From birth, we are all trying to make sense of the world. Babies and Children spend much of their time gathering information and creating ideas, opinions and coming to conclusions based on their own unique experiences. They set themselves goals, explore different ways of achieving these goals, and understand when they have achieved them. Children view the world as a place of wonder and experimentation, they have natural curiosity and will constantly question how? what? when? who? where? and why?

We need to nurture and encourage this natural tendency, and work to create the ideal environment for thinking skills to flourish.

This book aims to:

- bring together information, theories and ideas about thinking skills;
- define what thinking skills are and why they are now considered so important;
- show how these key skills link with and are emphasised in current curriculum guidance;
- discuss the role of the adult;
- give ideas for setting up thinking and problem solving opportunities in settings and schools.

Have thinking skills been marginalised in recent times?

There is reference to thinking skills throughout the curriculum guidance and frameworks in England, Northern Ireland and Scotland. However when the UK government introduced age related tests in England, some teachers felt that the focus was being shifted from cross-curricular skills to separate subject knowledge. Publication of test results, target setting and the views held by some parents caused teachers to feel under pressure to teach in a far simpler, more directed way.

Some felt that the introduction of additional tests and curriculum content left no time for reflection or for deciding <u>how</u> subjects should be taught. There was a conviction (sadly unfounded) that each subject should be taught for a specific number of hours, and that seemed easier to achieve and provide evidence for if each subject had its own time space in the week. Some teachers then found it very difficult to maintain the cross curricular skills and elements that had been the 'glue' which gave the primary curriculum strength.

We were in danger of believing that thinking skills are only a theoretical part of the National Curriculum and that, in practice, thinking is being pushed aside in the need to teach facts and knowledge that can be tested easily - that teaching is more important than learning! However, as we will explore, thinking skills are still very much alive in curriculm guidance currently being implemented.

The importance of thinking skills

Thinking about thinking skills at every stage in children's learning can help us to:

- give children the time and space they need to discover the world in which they live;

- recognise how important it is to treat children as individuals who progress at different rates - not just in relation to their age;

- ensure that parents know and understand that education is not purely about facts and rote learning;

- provide children with transferable skills - in enquiry, information processing, reasoning, evaluation, problem solving and creative thinking - that they can use in order to achieve in all areas throughout their time in school and beyond.

Early learning about thinking is crucial and can change children's lives!

The early years are so important because most of the growth of the brain occurs in early childhood. By the age of six, the brain in the majority of children is ninety percent of its adult size. It is vital that we introduce and encourage thinking skills at this stage rather than waiting until later when brain development has slowed.

This book offers and extends advice and ideas to include practice in Key Stage 1, because recent research about transition from the Foundation Stage shows that children need to continue to learn through practical experiences throughout the primary age range. One of the consistent messages from research is how important these years are for building the foundations of social, emotional, physical and intellectual development.

Offering experiences and opportunities for developing thinking skills is vital in early childhood settings and in schools. The human brain can only hold a limited amount of unconnected information for future use, so a knowledge based curriculum is bound to fail in the longer term, because children's brains cannot absorb and retain information in this form.

Society and its associated technology are changing rapidly, people need transferable skills, and they need to be able to use these skills in different contexts to solve problems. We have more information, and many more ways of accessing such information than ever before, and therefore need to be able to gather this in a coherent way before making judgements and decisions. Children need thinking skills to be a natural part of their lives so they can take full advantage of the world in which they are growing up. If we can help children to develop their skills in thinking and reasoning, these skills will last a lifetime, and take children beyond just pressing buttons to get information, but thinking creatively about what the information means for them, and how they can use it. Our future lies in the hands of our children - let's give them the skills they need.

Sustained shared thinking

Sustained shared thinking is most recently analysed and described in the Effective Provision of Pre-school (EPPE) research. This project (Europe's largest longitudinal investigation into the effects

of pre-school education on children's developmental outcomes at the start of primary school) was initiated in 1997 and is due to continue at least until 2008, examined good practice in pre-schools and is tracking the progress of the the original cohort into their primary schools.

In this work, 'sustained shared thinking' is identified as one of the key features of high quality provision, and is described in the following way:

'Sustained shared thinking' is where two or more individuals 'work together' in an intellectual way to solve a problem, clarify a concept, evaluate an activity, extend a narrative etc. Both parties must contribute to the thinking and it must develop and extend the understanding.

It was found that the most effective settings encourage 'sustained shared thinking' which was most likely to occur when children were interacting 1:1 with an adult or with a single peer partner. It would appear that periods of 'sustained shared thinking' are a necessary pre-requisite for the most effective early years practice.

EPPE Report, Institute of Education, London

The research also found that in high quality provision:

- adult 'modelling' is often combined with sustained periods of shared thinking;
- open-ended questioning is also associated with better cognitive achievement (however, even in high quality settings, open ended questioning made up only 5% of questioning);
- the balance of who initiated the activities, staff or child, was about equal, children were encouraged to initiate activities as often as the staff;
- the extent to which staff extended child-initiated interactions was important. Almost half of the child-initiated episodes which contained intellectual challenge, included interventions from a staff member to extend the child's thinking.

Sustained shared thinking and critical thinking are now key elements of the new Early Years Foundation Stage (2007).

This book contains advice and guidance to help you to enhance the thinking that is going on already in your school or setting, by thinking about thinking yourself, looking for the things you are already doing, observing what the babies and children are already doing, and understanding what is happening. Thinking skills are here to stay!

Using this book

This book is for all those working with children from birth to eight years, but the principles have application over a wide range of ages and situations. Starting on thinking when children are very young is far better than trying to initiate these skills when children have become used to behaving and learning in other ways.

Developing our own understanding of thinking skills and the types of activities that aid children in their development of these skills can help us to help children in all areas of their learning.

Part One of this book offers information on **what thinking skills are**. It includes an overview of some theoretical approaches towards thinking skills, how they feature in children's learning and the curriculum, and ways to help the children you work with to develop these skills.

Part One also includes information on how these key skills develop, and the place of thinking skills and sustained shared thinking in curriculum documentation from birth to around the age of seven.

You will also find sections on the role of the adult, nurturing the skills, and how to provide an environment for thinking in your setting or school.

Part Two has **examples of investigations and challenges** to get babies and children thinking, and help to develop their skills in this area. These investigations and challenges may make you think as well! The suggested activities provide you with starting points for extending independent exploration

and, using the resources available to you in your individual situation. The activities are only a starting point, as opportunities for developing thinking through investigations and challenges are endless.

Remember, sustaining thinking skills does not need special equipment, space or additional time. It just needs commitment from you, and a will to make it happen.

Part 1 - Thinking About Thinking Skills

- What are 'Thinking Skills', and what is 'Sustained Shared Thinking'?

- Major theories and research into thinking

- Thinking skills in the UK education system, from Birth to Three to the end of Key Stage 1

- How do thinking skills develop?

- The role of the adult in sustaining thinking

- Nurturing thinking by nurturing the child

- Using language to expand thinking

- Providing a thinking environment

What are thinking skills?

- Thinking skills are more than an acquisition of knowledge, they include an element of knowing, thinking about and discussing thinking. This is referred to as metacognition.

- Thinking skills encourage children to learn to think for themselves.

- Thinking skills are supported by learning for real reasons in a highly motivating environment.

- Thinking skills are usually divided into six areas -

    enquiry skills

    information processing skills

    reasoning skills

    evaluation skills

    problem solving skills

    creative skills

    - all of which are interrelated and complement each other.

- Thinking skills do not have a hierarchical order, none is more or less important than any other, and we often use more than one at a time. They need to be nurtured and developed alongside each other in a practical, meaningful way.

Enquiry skills

Enquiry skills enable the learner to ask questions, something that children are already very keen to do, and babies do it from the moment they are born. They may not be able to articulate their questions, but are continually seeking answers to make sense of the world. Enquiry skills allow the learner to develop questions which are relevant or specific to a subject, where answers help the learner to plan more questions and research, gathering information in a way that they and others can understand.

Asking questions seems like a simple skill, but the use of and the understanding of questions is acquired over time. Children need opportunities to ask and answer different types of questions for different reasons, and this happens better when adults model different sorts of questioning.

Information processing skills

Information processing skills enable the learner to do something with information they have gathered by asking and answering questions. They then need the processing skills to organise and retain the most relevant information in a way which relates to the subject and makes sense to them. To do this the learner needs to be able to see links between the different pieces of information.

These skills appear to be very complicated and technical, but they develop over time and begin as babies use their senses to explore and make sense of the world.

Reasoning skills

Reasoning skills enable the learner to form an opinion based on the questions, answers, experiences and information they have. The child gradually acquires the skills needed to verbalise these thoughts and explain to others how they came to their decisions or opinions. Of course, these skills are closely linked to both language development and social and emotional development. We often see very young children display frustration in behaviour when they are unable to explain their ideas or opinions to others. It is important that the learner has the opportunities to develop these skills alongside the relevant language, emotional and social skills, and that these are modelled by older children and adults. (The EPPE Research found that children from socially disadvantaged backgrounds are less likely to have had these skills and the associated language modelled at home).

Evaluation skills

Evaluation skills enable the learner to look at information they receive, think about it's relevance and decide whether they agree with it or not. They develop the ability to devise informal, then more formal criteria for judging information and their findings, to help them to be clear about what they have found out or decided. They learn to be aware of what they are aiming to achieve and what this may look like, so they can be confident in their own judgements and opinions, enabling them to know when they have achieved their objective to the best of their ability.

Problem solving skills

The ability to recognise that something can be changed and will make a difference to the present situation is the beginning of problem solving, and recognising the existence of the problem is just the beginning of being able to solve it! The learner needs to develop a range of strategies they can use to solve the problem. Questioning is one of these strategies.

Once strategies have been tried and practiced, the learner needs to be able to observe, evaluate and decide whether they have achieved the solution they wanted. They must also develop an awareness that their solution may not be the only one.

Creative thinking skills

Creative thinking skills enable the learner to look for alternatives, not always accepting the first answer. Through experience they will realise that there are many ways to discover, explore and find out about the world. The learner develops the ability to look beyond the obvious, acquiring the confidence to create new ideas and change methods. Creative thinking allows the learner to look for different outcomes and to recognise that what they thought would happen may change. Creative thinking skills are often more about the process of the learning journey than about the product. When trying new methods the learner needs to develop the confidence not to be afraid to make mistakes or try alternatives, understanding that trial and error are both vital elements in success.

Creative thinking is the ability to use the imagination to invent something new and to generate new ideas. Sometimes these ideas are truly new and sometimes they are old ideas, implemented in a new situation. These ideas may be very practical or they may not. When the ideas are not suitable, a real creative thinker will be prepared to go back to the drawing board.

When looking at the nature of these skills it does seem apparent that they are essential for developing dispositions for learning, they are also very closely linked to social development and communication.

Sustained Shared Thinking

It is now clear from research and observations of practice that children whose thinking skills have been nurtured in the company of supportive adults will do better than children whose thinking has developed alone or in the company of their peers.

It seems that the way that sensitive adults (practitioners, parents, teachers and other mentors) will naturally respond to children is the key to turning adult contribution to children's play into real sustained shared thinking. The adults may not know the names of the different skills, they often use them instinctively, but their part in the process now appears to be vital.

Key components are:
- trust and confidence between the partners in the situation
- the use of the language of thinking (defined in the EPPE research as *'two or more individuals working together in an intellectual way to solve a problem, clarify a concept, evaluate an activity, extend a narrative etc. Both parties must contribute to the thinking and it must develop and extend the understanding.'*) The best sustained thinking observed in the research was in 1-1 situations with an adult or single peer partner.
- substantial periods of time to think, talk and engage with the task
- genuine shared ownership of the process, where tasks initiated by children are given equal respect and time as those initiated by adults
- open questions and flexible language
- modelling of the thinking skills by adults
- the children's language and thinking is extended by the adults through questioning and modelling of skills.

In effective settings, the balance of who initiated the activities, staff or child, was about equal, children were encouraged to initiate activities as often as the staff. Similarly in effective settings the extent to which staff extended child-initiated interactions was important. Almost half of the child-initiated episodes which contained intellectual challenge, included interventions from a staff member to extend the child's thinking.

EPPE Report; 2005

Some Major Theories and Thinkers

The perceived usefulness of thinking skills as instruments for curriculum development has fluctuated over the years, usually as a result of the stance of any one particular government at the time.

The importance given to them is inclined to occur when more formal approaches to learning are perceived to have failed.

Peter Vass, Oxford Brookes University (2002)

Many different methods for the teaching of thinking have been used and assessed across the UK in the last few years. Here is a sample of different ways 'thinking' has been taught.

Theory	Founder	Summary
Instrumental Enrichment	Reuvan Feuerstein	Learning how to learn - through discussion and group work, not rote and reproduction.
Philosophy for children - Thinking through Stories	Matthew Lipman	Providing children with stories that promote thinking gives them the opportunities and freedom to think for themselves.
Thinking Hats	Edward De Bono	By learning to understand how emotions effect their thought process, children can develop their creative and logical thinking.
TASC (Thinking Actively in a Social Context)	Wallace and Adams	Focuses on problem solving - the importance of breaking a problem down into pre assigned stages in order to work through it.
Thinking through Primary Teaching	Steve Higgins	Instigators in developing subject specific thinking skills, so that teachers can integrate them into their lessons.
ACTS (Activating Children's Thinking Skills)	Carol McGuiness	Believes that the development of thinking skills in children involves whole school changes and cross-curricular teaching.

Instrumental Enrichment

Many educationalists have been interested in the work carried out by Reuvan Feuerstein, who was involved with young immigrants after World War Two. These youngsters suffered traumatic early lives and few had experience of education or normal family life. Their IQ test results were so low that many thought them to be ineducable.

Feuerstein worked on methods to discover what cognitive abilities these young people were lacking and how these could be stimulated. He devised a set of techniques called 'Instrumental Enrichment', based on learning how to be a learner. Although his methods predict the learning potential of a person they also brought the idea of learning to learn and what makes a learner to the attention of educationalists.

Much of the method involves group learning through discussions as well as pencil and paper methods. It is not however learning through rote or a reproduction of a skill. It involves the application of rules and strategies, and it enables students to see problems, make connections, motivate themselves and improve their learning capacity.

Philosophy for children - Thinking through Stories

Matthew Lipman, a philosophy professor, believed that children are born 'philosophers' because they are naturally curious and questioning of the world. He felt that education had taught them facts and people in authority had taught them opinions, but no one had taught them to think for themselves.

Lipman believed that children need starting points for their enquiries and the freedom to explore, so he decided to develop a method to promote thinking skills in young children. The programme he and his colleagues devised is called 'Philosophy for Children'. It is based on stories that have been written to promote thinking, questioning and discussion. These stories have been used in many countries to aid children's ability to reason and discuss.

Lipman's research suggest that skills have improved and been generalised across the curriculum, because the children involved in this method have been learning to think.

A TES article on 'Thinking through Stories' in Key Stage One (20/6/03) discusses Lipman's theory. In the article a teacher notes that in these sessions the children are more thoughtful, better at asking questions, more patient with listening and more creative with their ideas and judgements. You can find more about Philosophy for Children by using a search engine, or using the DfES website and searching for Thinking Skills.

De Bono's Thinking Hats

Edward De Bono is well known for his theories on lateral thinking, creative thinking, mind mapping and parallel thinking. He has written 62 books about the development of thinking and thinking skills.

In 2005 De Bono posed this question to all Education Authorities ⟶

"Which parts of the school curriculum directly develop the thinking required for constructive thinking, design thinking, creative thinking and operational thinking?"

One of De Bono's methods used for teaching thinking skills in schools is called 'Six Thinking Hats'. The six thinking hats are colour coded and relate to different sorts of thinking:

- white for information gathering;
- red for feelings and gut reactions;
- black for negative points;
- yellow for positive points;
- green for creativity and new ideas;
- blue for organising and planning.

During the sessions, the children usually work in a group to solve problems and are encouraged to use one colour hat at a time. Once they are familiar with the process, they are able to apply this method of working to working on their own as well as to group work, as taking part in the activity helps them to become aware of the different aspects of their thinking when problem solving or analysing.

However most of the material using the Six Hats process has been developed for children aged five and over, as it is hoped that older children will understand how emotional reactions can cloud good reasoning, and that it is essential to understand others' feelings about an issue in order to reach a conclusion.

TASC (Thinking Actively in a Social Context)

Wallace and Adams (1993) developed this model based on problem solving. The framework can be used by teachers to explore problems relevant to their children and situation. It involves breaking the problem down into a series of steps in order to find a solution.

The steps in the process are:

- gather and organise what is known already;
- identify the problem;
- generate as many ideas as possible;
- decide which idea many be the best;
- implement this idea;
- evaluate the results, including thinking whether it could be done in a better way;
- communicate the ideas to others, thinking about the best way to do this.

There is an emphasis on working in small groups and the importance of social learning, and the theory is explored in several books for early years practitioners.

Thinking through Primary Teaching

This theory was constructed by Steve Higgins who has taught children in KS1 and KS2. Higgins is now a key member of the Thinking Skills Research Centre and part of the Primary PGCE Team at Newcastle University. The Research Centre has been involved in monitoring and evaluating many different methods and programmes for the teaching of thinking. One of the developments has been to work on subject specific thinking skills, enabling teachers to integrate thinking skills into their lessons. Thinking through Primary Teaching was tried in a number of schools before publication to the wider educational community.

ACTS (Activating Children's Thinking Skills)

ACTS is a project established to increase children's thinking in KS2. It was devised in Northern Ireland and co-ordinated by Carol McGuiness and her team at Queens University, Belfast.

The programme consists of a handbook of example lessons and training for teachers, with an emphasis on cross-curricular skill development rather than specific thinking skills lessons. The range of key skills covered is comprehensive and developing a language to talk about thinking is a key element.

As the project developed it became apparent that a shift in perception from developing thinking skills to establishing thinking classrooms would be a key feature. The design, resources and teachers' beliefs about learning needed to adapt to enable children to 'think about thinking'. Aspects of time and curriculum restraints caused problems for teachers, but all those involved acknowledged benefits for the children and the schools.

Carol McGuiness has taken this viewpoint further in her book *From Thinking Skills to Thinking Classrooms*. In this book she states that children can take control of their own learning when teachers concentrate on how the children learn rather than looking solely at what they are learning. McGuiness believes that thinking skills can be embedded into and across the curriculum, but that teachers need support and an understanding of the importance of thinking for this to happen effectively.

Her work in early thinking, and her construct for developing thinking skills has affected the framework for the Early Years Enriched Curriculum in Northern Ireland, which has thinking skills and personal capabilities as key features. She doesn't see the process as a linear pattern, but as a collection of tools for learning, described in a diagram like this:

Most attempts to teach thinking skills are based on some formal analysis of the nature of thinking, but what they are all trying to achieve, irrespective of their precise theoretical foundations, is to develop the person's thinking to a qualitatively higher level.

Carol McGuinness (1999)

Numerous methods and programmes have been developed and used in the UK and across the world to develop metacognition and thinking skills, but they are mostly for children over the age of 5 years and more commonly for children who are in KS2.

Three key elements seem to be present in the majority of methods -

- The place of spoken language
- The importance of giving time to discussion
- Problem solving linked to children's interests and relevant activities

To achieve these three elements children need to be given the opportunity to develop the social and emotional skills that underpin them.

Most of these methods are subject specific or lesson plans to be used for a set amount of time, but as the ACTS research project shows, thinking skills can be cross-curricular, and should be founded in thinking classrooms where adults and children work together in sustained shared thinking.

In 2004, the Chief Inspector of schools and the Director of the Basic Skills Agency voiced concerns about the poor language, behavioural and social skills of 5 year olds. (TES 2004)

'What is needed now is for all those who work with babies and young children to promote thinking skills as part of everyday experience. To realise that thinking begins at birth and not see it as an 'add on' lesson or as a method to use for a set time with older children'.

No longer is it enough to see our children as empty vessels to be filled up with facts, skills and knowledge. Instead we can see our pupils as unlit fires, just waiting for us to spark the touch paper and ignite an interest in thinking about how and why the world around them works.

Sue Cowley; Create a Thinking Classroom; Scholastic; 2006

Thinking Skills in the Curriculum

Thinking skills do not suddenly begin to develop when children enter school at age five, they begin as soon as the child is born. Thinking is obviously a concept that we are familiar with, however some people may not have been aware of thinking skills or what is meant by this. Thankfully, since the review by Carol McGuiness in 1998 and the explicit inclusion of thinking skills in the National Curriculum, interest in the teaching of thinking skills has burgeoned in the UK.

In this section you will see where thinking skills link with and appear in the national guidance for Birth to Three, the Foundation Stage and Key Stage One.

Birth to Three Framework

The Birth to Three Framework embraces the concept of children learning to learn through the promotion of opportunities and experiences that involve thinking. Although, from 2008, the new Early Years Foundation Stage Guidance replaced both Birth to Three Matters and the Curriculum Guidance for the Foundation Stage, both these documents still remain core references for practitioners working with Children from birth to five.

Looking first at the principles that underpin the Birth to Three Matters Framework, these are the ones that relate to thinking:

- Babies and young children are social beings, they are competent learners from birth.

- Learning is a shared process and children learn most effectively when, with the support of a knowledgeable and trusted adult, they are actively engaged and interested.

- Children learn when they are given appropriate responsibility, allowed to make errors, decisions and choices, and respected as autonomous and competent learners.

- Children learn by doing rather than by being told.

Of the Four Aspects of the Framework, two relate directly to thinking: A Skilful Communicator and A Competent Learner.

Within the text about A Skilful Communicator, there are many words which describe how babies and young children can offered opportunities for thinking. These include:

- exploring, experimenting, labelling, expressing
- describing, questioning, representing, predicting
- sharing thoughts, feelings and ideas
- influencing others
- negotiating and making choices.

Within A Competent Learner all the statements can contribute to early thinking. However, some words demonstrate clearly how young children begin their lifelong journey of learning. Words such as:

- explore
- experiment
- discover
- imagine
- create

There are also elements of thinking in A Strong Child:

- realising that s/he is separate and different from others
- recognising personal characteristics and preferences
- finding out what s/he can do
- becoming confident in what s/he can do
- valuing individuality and the contributions of self and others
- having a role and identity within a group.

And in A Healthy Child:

This Framework gives us such good starting points for learning how to learn, and for developing the attitudes and skills needed to be a competent and creative thinker.

- being able to express feelings
- demonstrating personal preferences
- learning about rules
- making decisions.
- knowing when and how to ask for help

The Foundation Stage Curriculum

The Curriculum Guidance for the Foundation Stage is also packed with references to thinking skills.

Principles which form the basis for the guidance include:

- Children are entitled to provision that supports and extends knowledge, skills, understanding and confidence.
- Early years experience should build on what children already know and can do. It should also encourage a positive attitude and disposition to learn.
- Children need time to become engrossed, work in depth and complete activities of their own choosing.
- The environment should provide the structure for teaching within which the children explore, experiment, plan and make decisions for themselves, thus enabling them to learn and develop.

These principles underpin the need for children to continue to be engaged in activities that encourage and develop thinking beyond the earliest stages.

The Foundation Stage Curriculum is built on learning through play as there is much research to shows this is the most effective method of learning.

The benefits of learning through play are clearly stated in the guidance, for example, through play children can 'think creatively and imaginatively' and 'communicate with others as they investigate or solve problems'. Both of these statements link directly with the thinking skills described in 'What are thinking skills?' on page 7 of the Guidance.

Thinking skills approaches are emerging as a powerful means of engaging teachers and pupils in improving the quality of learning in classrooms.

DfES Standards Site (2005)

The curriculum in the Foundation Stage is divided into six areas of learning, each broken down into more specific learning strands. Development is tracked through stepping stones in learning which lead to a set of early learning goals.

Much of the language used in the stepping stones and goals echoes the move towards the early development of thinking skills and thoughtful attitudes. Language included here builds on Birth to Three Matters by using the following words and phrases:

- motivated to learn
- confident to try new ideas
- initiative
- experience
- explore
- examine

- investigate
- communicate
- relationships
- understand
- consequences
- independently
- respect

- negotiate
- question
- modify
- organise
- problem solve
- curiosity
- respond.

There is a whole strand of development dedicated to 'dispositions and attitudes' that relates entirely to thinking skills, and this strand builds to goals that include:

- Continues to be interested, motivated and excited to learn;
- Is confident to try new activities, initiate ideas and speak in a familiar group;
- Maintains attention and concentrates;
- Sustains involvement and perseveres, particularly when trying to solve a problem or reach a satisfactory conclusion.

Practitioners in the Foundation Stage are now expected to collect 80% of the evidence used to complete the Foundation Stage Profile in child-initiated activities, giving even more emphasis on the need to develop thinking skills and independent learning.

The Early Years Foundation Stage

As the Birth to Three Matters and Foundation Stage Guidance documents began to become embedded in practice, it became evident that the links between the two were unclear, particularly as Children reached the age of three. This proved difficult for practitioners who were trying to provide for a continuous curriculum experience within and between settings. The Guidance was updated in April 2007 to combine these frameworks into a continuous progression from birth to the end of the the year in which the child becomes five.

This new Guidance is intended to support and expand previous documentation by amplifying the guidance for practitioners and providing a set of developmental statements in a progression. These statements are accompanied by guidance on observation, effective practice and planning and resourcing. For our purposes in this book, we have concentrated here on the guidance within the new framework for ensuring that the development of thinking skills (referred to as Critical Thinking) is ensured.

The print documents are in three parts, accompanied by a poster and material on CD-RoM.

The Statutory Guidance emphasises personalisation of learning, ensuring that the early years curriculum fits the child, not making the child fit the curriculum. Personalised learning is described thus: Providers must plan and organise their systems to ensure that every child receives an enjoyable and challenging learning and development experience that is tailored to meet their individual needs.

This part of the guidance also outlines the goals for learning, which are the statutory assessment criteria, and remain in the most part unchanged from those used within the Foundation Stage Guidance. The goals associated with thinking skills, which have been included previously in this section remain unchanged, and some are now being identified as being the key goals for lifelong learning.

The Non-Statutory Guidance has a substantial and complex introduction to the Framework, and includes the first specific guidance to be offered nationally to early years practitioners on Sustained Shared Thinking (Page 9), features of which are described as:

- adults are aware of the children's interests and understandings and the adults and children work together to develop an idea or skill;
- in the most effective settings practitioners support and challenge children's thinking by getting involved in the thinking process with them;
- there are positive trusting relationships between adults and children;
- the adults show genuine interest, offer encouragement, clarify ideas and ask open questions which supports and extends children's thinking and helps them to make connections in learning.

The document also contains guidance on how the curriculum should be organised, planned and resourced, and gives details of the developmental stages in six areas of learning across six broad and overlapping developmental stages. Each stage is accompanied by guidance on how to observe the learning, what effective practice might look like, and how practitioners might plan for and resource the learning. Statements linked to sustained shared thinking, taken from various sections of the document include:

In Dispositions and Attitudes

- Devote uninterrupted time to babies when you can play with them. Be attentive and fully focused.
- Give time for children to pursue their learning without interruption, and return to activities.
- Encourage children to explore and talk about what they are learning, valuing their ideas and ways of doing things.

In Language for Communication

- Provide practical experiences that encourage children to ask and respond to questions, for example, explaining pulleys or wet and dry sand.
- Encourage children to predict possible endings to stories and events.
- Set up collaborative tasks... Help children to talk about and plan how they will begin, what parts each will play and what materials they will need.

In Language for Thinking

- Use talk to describe what children are doing by providing a running commentary.

- Help children to predict and order events coherently, by providing props and materials that encourage children to re-enact, using talk and action.

- Ask children to think in advance about how they will accomplish a task. Talk through and sequence the stages together.

In Exploration and Investigation

- Provide opportunities to observe things closely through a variety of means, including magnifiers and photographs.

- Encourage children to raise questions and suggest solutions and answers.

- Encourage children to speculate on the reasons why things happen and how things work.

In Designing and Making

- Provide a range of tools, for example, scissors, hole punch, stapler, junior hacksaw, glue spreader, rolling, pin, cutter, knife, grater, and encourage children to handle them carefully and use their correct names.

- Provide opportunities for children to practice skills, initiate and plan simple projects, and find their own solutions in the design and make process.

These are just a few of the many helpful suggestions for good practice in early years settings, and would also provide a useful basis for looking at the provision in Key Stage 1.

The Principles into Practice Cards provide information about effective practice across the four themes of the EYFS - A Unique Child, Positive Relationships, Enabling Environments and Learning and Development. Thinking Skills are emphasised throughout, but particular reference is made in Learning and Development (the yellow cards) where language for thinking, problem solving, play and exploration, active learning and creativity and critical thinking are all addressed. The following statement appears on the card entitled Supporting Learning:

Warm, trusting relationships with knowledgeable adults support children's learning more effectively than any amount of resources.

The key role of the adult is explored later in this section.

Sustained Shared Thinking in the Early Years Foundation Stage

Within the Early Years Foundation Stage Practice Guidance (2007), sustained shared thinking is described in these words:

A high quality, continuously improving setting will provide:

Sustained shared thinking, which means:

- adults are aware of the children's interests and understandings and the adults and children work together to develop an idea or skill;
- in the most effective settings practitioners support and challenge children's thinking by getting involved in the thinking process with them;
- there are positive trusting relationships between adults and children;
- the adults show genuine interest, offer encouragement, clarify ideas and ask open questions which supports and extends children's thinking and helps them to make connections in learning.

Features of sustained shared thinking:

An instructive learning environment

Clear routines

Free choice

Appropriate intervention from adults

One to one experiences with an adult or single peer partner

Extended child-initiated play, coupled with the provision of teacher initiated group work

EPPE

National Curriculum - Key Stage One

The National Curriculum includes aims for the school curriculum. Within these aims are references to thinking, such as:

- The school curriculum should develop enjoyment of learning.
- The curriculum should enable pupils to think creatively and critically and to solve problems.

Thinking skills are highlighted within the Guidance in the section on Promoting Skills Across the National Curriculum. It states that the skills of information processing, reasoning, enquiry, creative thinking and evaluation are embedded in the curriculum.

In the Programmes of Study (DfES 2000) there are constant references to thinking related aims. These appear particularly in the Breadth of Study sections, where opportunities for working in groups, working in a practical manner, exploration, applying their skills and knowledge, evaluating, investigating and communicating are recommended. Teachers should revisit this guidance for a refreshing view of what the national Curriculum is intended to provide.

In 2004 the Primary National Strategy sent a comprehensive staff training pack based on the findings and conclusions in the *Excellence and Enjoyment: a strategy for primary schools* (May 2003) report to all Primary Schools.

This pack is for staff training on:

- Understanding how learning develops
- Creating a learning culture
- And, planning and assessment for learning

It consists of booklets with ideas for training, video, and DVD materials to use as a staff team. One of the booklets is concerned with the key aspects of learning - Thinking Skills.

Recent Developments

Since the revision of the National Curriculum in 2000, there have been other developments in providing support for schools from the DfES and other government supported bodies. The contacts for some of these are:

www.standards.dfes.gov.uk/thinkingskills

> 'The aim of this website therefore is to provide information for classroom teachers working in primary schools in the UK about thinking skills programmes and approaches that are currently available. Background information to thinking skills approaches, the compilation of the database and some case studies of how schools have used the thinking skills to develop teaching and learning are included.'

www.literacytrust.org.uk

> Contains updates, research, resources, case studies on Thinking Skills development.

www.teachernet.gov.uk

> Information about Philosophy for Children.

www.ncaction.org.uk/creativity

> 'This website gives practical ideas on how to promote pupils' creative thinking and behaviour'

www.qca.org.uk

> Click through to Customise your Curriculum.

> 'See examples of how teachers are taking ownership of the curriculum, shaping it and making it their own.'

Where we have put inverted commas, this is the website's own wording.

How do thinking skills develop?

There are six types of thinking skills - Enquiry Skills, Information Processing Skills, Reasoning Skills, Evaluation Skills, Problem Solving Skills and Creative Skills. In this section we will take a close look at each type, alongside case studies of situations where babies and children are displaying the use of these skills. Although we are looking at each area separately, they are of course interconnected, and when thinking we draw on many areas of thinking, often simultaneously.

Enquiry Skills

Enquiry skills are linked with communication and understanding. Asking questions may appear to be a simple skill, but the type of question asked and understood is refined with age and experience. The development of enquiry skills can be seen in the language a child uses and the reason for their question.

Babies are asking questions about the world with their senses as soon as they are born. They need a variety of experiences and opportunities to develop good enquiry links in the brain. From about the age of 5 months babies use hand gestures to make requests - a hand stretch and a look says - 'I want that - get it for me'. Although there is no question mark, it is the beginning of asking.

Between 16-24 months toddlers use name words with a questioning tone - they are seeking answers to 'is it a...?' or 'what?', before they know the question word 'what?'. At 18 months a child may say 'more' and use a physical prop such as a cup or bowl. At two years old - 'help me?' or 'up?' with a pleading tone and gesture to whatever s/he needs help with. These enquiry words continue to become more advanced with experience, support and encouragement.

'Where?' is usually the first questioning word to appear, at around two, and this is closely followed by 'what?' and 'who?', three and four years olds have usually added 'why?' and 'when?', and by five years old children are beginning to realise that there is a range of ways to use questions to find out more about something they are interested in.

Older children will ask more specific and complicated questions related to a topic or investigation, and need to be introduced to 'what if', 'how?', 'how well?' and the more complex versions of 'why?' to predict, investigate and evaluate projects and tasks. They will then begin to think about the type of question that they need to ask to make sure they get the information they need.

Case study - Enquiry Skills

A systematic or scientific process for answering questions and solving problems based on gathering evidence through observation, analysis and reflection.

Matty is exploring a box of tadpoles. He is using his senses of touch and vision to explore something he has never seen before. He calls an adult over to ask them about his discovery.

'Wassat?' he asks.

'They are tadpoles'

' Mmm. 'wimming.'

'Yes, they are swimming,' says the practitioner.

'Touchit?' says Matty.

'Yes you can touch it very gently, but don't pick them up.'

'Wiggling!' says Matty with excitement.

'Wassat?' poking the remaining frogspawn in the bowl.

'They are eggs. Look, they've got little tadpoles inside. I wonder if they will come out.'

'Baby ones, coming out?'

'Yes they will come out soon, when they are ready.'

'I wait here,' says Matty as he squats down beside the bowl to watch some more.

The provision of a range of stimulating outdoor experiences has prompted Matty's enquiry.

Note how the adult supports Matty's questions by echoing what he says, and adding manageable amounts of information in simple and relevant language.

For this two year old, information about frogs may not be necessary at this stage. His interest is in the here and now. He can follow what comes next as he watches the tadpoles over the next few days.

A two year old may use questions as a means of getting or sustaining attention, but as children become more aware of the power of questions, they begin to ask the questions which help them to make sense of all that they are experiencing. Four year olds often use the 'why?' question repeatedly in order to have some control over what they are being asked to do, rather than to seek or collect information.

Information Processing Skills

Babies begin to make sense of information gathered through the senses from the moment they are born. In fact, many claim that their sense of hearing is gathering information while they are forming in the womb. As they gain experience and repeatedly react to things in certain ways they develop feelings about them. They can then begin to organise information. Tastes, for example, are organised into pleasant tastes and unpleasant tastes - things they want in their mouths and things they don't. This information is eventually gathered together and known as food, or not food depending on what a baby has brought to his/her mouth.

Toddlers are obsessed with naming - categorising information into types - 'brum brums' become cars, lorries, and buses. They have different names but the toddler knows they belong together. A toddler who is always pointing, saying 'Uhh' is most probably not saying they want what they are pointing at, they are most probably asking you to name the object or person they are pointing at - pointing is a powerful way of seeking information.

Young children often have an area of interest that becomes an area of expertise, such as diggers, dinosaurs, farm animals, sharks, minibeasts. They ask questions and collect information endlessly about their subject because it interests them. They remember information related to their interests although they may not remember other, sometimes much simpler, information that adults think is important!

Building on these interests is a useful way to develop thinking skills - relevance is a key to motivation and memory, so practitioners and teachers should watch and note children's interests.

Older children continue to seek more information about a particular object or subject. They are able to sort the relevant information from the irrelevant and ask more specific questions. More mature children will begin to use books and other sources and to make connections between the different pieces of information they discover.

Case study - Information processing skills

Collecting information, making links between the different pieces, and beginning to come to conclusions.

Callum is six. He has found the backbone of an animal while out on a walk with his family. He is fascinated and sure it is the backbone of a dinosaur - dinosaurs are his passion!

He holds the bones carefully as he manipulates them to find out how they move. He fires endless questions at his family about how the bones work, how they got in the field, where the rest of the skeleton is, what sort of dinosaur they might be from, where the head fixed on, and so on.

As his family answer his questions, he begins to think about what he is learning. If these are the bones of a dinosaur, how big would the dinosaur be? Are the bones too small for a really scary dinosaur like the ones he loves?

The bones are taken home, then to school, as Callum continues to find out about them. With help from his teacher and parents, he uses books and the internet to try to establish which animal the bones belong to, eventually putting them in a box with a carefully written label saying:

Callum's family are very understanding. They know he is fascinated with dinosaurs and are prepared to help him find out whether he has found some dinosaur bones.

Asking and answering questions are key features of information gathering and processing. Most Children think better aloud, and need time to keep returning to the information over and over again as they process it.

'I fownd thse bones in a fild. I fot it was a dinosaur, but it is a ships bones from a dead ship'
Callum 2007

Reasoning Skills

Reasoning skills are linked with language, but also with social and emotional development. Children need to feel confident, relaxed and engaged before they can begin to link information together into conclusions about experiences or possibilities. Reasoning is also about generalising what is known, so the knowledge can be applied in other situations and activities, creating a map of knowledge that can enable a child to make sense of the world.

Babies are able to make simple decisions and come to initial conclusions about basic likes and dislikes based on their experiences. They will express their opinions verbally and physically, but it is up to an adult to interpret and work out why the baby does or does not like something.

2-3 year olds often display tantrums. These often result from their inability to make their views and opinions understood. The decisions toddlers make and the views they express are not always based on a huge amount of gathered information, but they are firmly held and often violently expressed. Toddlers are beginning to learn about the consequences of their own and others' actions - and getting an early experience of the skill of reasoning. Parents of toddlers often become masters of negotiation from necessity, and in reasoning and explaining to their toddler why certain things must happen, they are modelling the verbal and reasoning skills their child will need to learn in order to develop good social and thinking skills.

As children reach 5-6 years old they have had more experience of what the consequences of actions are likely to be, but this does not necessarily mean they accept them any more easily! Tantrums, sulks and arguments are often a continuing feature of children's struggles with their emotions and attempts to understand their place in the world. Even though they are more aware of the need for their opinions to be based on information and/or experience, they may still revert to the 'Why?' response when frustrated, even though in most situations they can understand the need to take the views and choices of others into consideration. Learning to listen to other people's opinions in a 'reasonable' way is sometimes a frustrating process.

Older children can use often use the information they have gathered through good enquiry skills to present a view or opinion, and explain their reasoning to others. By the age of seven, some (although by no means all) children will be able to listen to the opinions and suggestions of others and consider them as serious alternatives to their own. For others this skill takes a long time to develop.

A group of children are playing with shaving foam. They have never used it before.

The practitioner said 'Here is something new for you to use. What can you do with this?'

The children looked at the aerosol can and talked about what it could do and who had experience of one. Juan said 'My dad has this stuff with his shaver. I know how it works.'

'What is it?' said Maria, looking a bit doubtful.

'It's white stuff that squirts out,' says Juan.

'You do it then,' say the other children.

Juan squirts the foam into the tray. The other children are fascinated and delighted. They poke the foam with their fingers before getting deeply involved in finding out what it can do.

Later the same day, Maria is able to use her experiences to help other children who are starting to work with foam at a table.

The knowledge and information about what shaving foam can do quickly spreads through the class until, by the end of the week all the children are able to talk about their discoveries and describe the properties of foam, using relevant vocabulary, and taking turns to listen to each other.

Evaluation Skills

To evaluate information and experiences, and decide whether you have achieved your aim does not always require language or social skills, but to communicate and share what you have found out or created does. Babies and children are not consciously evaluating information, and neither are most of us as we go about our daily lives. We just have a general feeling that things are working out or not, and our personal resilience will enable us to evaluate what we do, and learn from mistakes as well as successes.

Babies evaluate the world in terms of comfort and discomfort. They know they have got the 'demand' right if they feel comfortable.

Toddlers can become very frustrated when they are unable to do something for themselves. They are evaluating their ability to use the information gathered and skills acquired to perform a task. They are not aware of the mental process, but they are very aware when they have done something they set out to do and distraught when they have not.

Young children often learn to evaluate what they have done by the reactions of others and it is important that they receive the right messages about their decisions and actions.

Children aged 4 - 5 will say 'I did it' with a huge smile and pride. They may not have vocalised or even thought out exactly what they wanted to do, but they know when they have achieved something special.

Helping children to understand that mistakes are part of learning, is a long job, fraught with difficulties and disappointments. However, through experience and modelling by others, both adults and peers, children begin to think about the criteria they need to determine success and to look positively on alternative solutions. As children become older they are able to look at what they do more critically and understand the usefulness of knowing what is needed to achieve an aim.

Experiences of shared challenges and sustained periods of child-initiated learning are the bedrock on which confident evaluation and resilience are built. This essential experience is even more effective if children's activities are valued and joined by adults who have the expertise to support and respond to children's thinking, using open questions and giving children plenty of time to explore and extend their interests. Evaluation can be effectively supported if the adults are involved in the processes of collecting and processing information, and reasoning about thinking.

This group of children spent over an hour constructing with CDs. There was no instruction, just the offer of the CDs to play with.

Cara started the line on the floor, and others joined her. She was careful to lay the CDs on the right side, with the shiny surface up, turning over any which were placed the wrong way up.

As the line of CDs grew, the children paused from time to time to decide where the line would go next, negotiating round and under furniture and other objects.

The adult who was working with them watched and acted as a sounding board, reflecting the ideas and comments of the children as they worked.

When the line was complete (and all the CDs used) the children were gently prompted to comment on their creation and how they had worked together to make it.

One child said 'Cara was bossy, she wanted the CDs her way round, but it looks nice now.'

Open ended resources and activities are more likely to stimulate creative and collaborative projects. Children respond enthusiastically to these resources, as long as they feel confident that adults are not expecting a predictable outcome, and will value all ideas and creations.

Problem Solving Skills

Can babies really solve problems? Yes! They need to problem solve in order to make sense of the world. It may not look like the problem solving that we recognise as adults, but it is. Babies are constantly trying to work out what things are, and they use all their senses to explore and gather information. They spend long periods examining their toes, wiggling them, tasting them, smelling them, feeling them. This helps them to decide what they are and who they belong to. They gather information and try out different senses in order to solve the problems they meet. After a while the fascination with their feet diminishes as they discover that they are a part of themselves!

As children grow, so do their strategies for solving problems. Some learn quickly that crying, hitting, or learned helplessness will encourage others to solve their problems for them. However, with encouragement, support, modelling and praise, most children learn a wide range of more acceptable problem solving strategies, and problem solving becomes more complex as these strategies are observed, experienced and tried with different sorts of problems.

Toddlers, renowned for their tempers, learn quickly that different strategies are needed for different situations. They are often frustrated when a method that worked when they wanted to make their ball move won't work on their bricks, or that the strategy they use with their parents will not work with their friends. Acquiring a range of problems solving strategies takes time and patience, and the best way to start is to make sure that children have plenty of relevant problems and challenges that are suited to their interests and maturity.

Young children can concentrate on a problem that interests them, such as how to get into the biscuit tin or making Lego pieces stay together, for a long time. Given plenty of time they will try a variety of methods and persevere until they succeed, and attention span will be extended if a supportive adult is available to talk them through what they are doing, or give a gentle bit of support.

When the problem is practical it is easy for children to decide when they have completed their task, but as they develop they are able to tackle more abstract problems, such as problems in stories. In these situations they need time to observe and discuss whether they have found a good solution. Well developed language skills are vital if children are to learn to discuss the problem and to listen to and understand others. Good social and emotional skills will also help with resilience and the ability to take suggestions and accept alternatives.

Case study - Problem solving

One morning, the children found these soft toys in a tree in the garden of their setting. Round the neck of one was a label reading:

> 'We fell from the sky.
> We have no names.
> We are hungry.'

The children were fascinated. They carefully took the toys out of the tree and brought them inside, read the label and talked about what they should do.

The discussion began with a decision on what the dogs could be called. Alternatives were listed by the adult and a vote was taken.

This decision quickly moved the children into making beds and a home for the dogs and discussing what dogs like to eat. Children who had pet dogs were very involved at this stage and showed a good knowledge of dogs' likes and dislikes.

How the dogs got in the bush stimulated some very innovative ideas, which included falling from a plane or balloon, being dropped by Father Christmas, blown by the wind or landing from the moon.

As the conversation developed, one child asked how they could find out who the dogs belonged to. Children suggested putting up notices in the community or advertising in the paper.

A group of children spent the whole day discussing and creating around the dogs who fell from the sky, who eventually starred in a popular photograph book about their adventures, made by the children.

Two weeks later the dogs disappeared, leaving a 'Thank you' note.

Stimulating problem solving and creativity is sometimes engineered by adults, who start the process by posing a problem in a familiar situation. This example is just one of the many ways that creative adults intrigue children into solving problems and finding solutions.

Why do you think the adults decided to remove the dogs after two weeks?

Creative Thinking

Using their imagination to solve problems, find information, present findings and come to surprising conclusions is the way in which most children naturally behave.

Young children make links between events and objects that we as adults find hard to understand. They can use one object to represent another in their play without any problems at all, and are not aware that this is creative thinking. Imaginary friends, Teddy Bears' picnics, being Superman, and making perfume from rose petals are all examples of young children's creative thinking skills.

Older children increase their capacity for creative thinking by developing these favourite themes into stories, not necessarily needing props to support their play and thinking. The ability to remain on task, to go back to the same task and try out new ideas helps with creativity, so children need time to develop these skills in play situations where they are involved in enjoyable activities that are meaningful to them.

Sustained thinking, alone, with friends or in the company of adults comes with age and experience, but even very young children can concentrate for long periods on self-initiated tasks.

Creative development occurs alongside all the other types of thinking, as long as creativity is encouraged and accepted, and not seen as annoying or deviating from what adults expect! Children will lose the ability to use creative thinking if others think their ideas are silly, or when over-formal education leaves no time for thought or individuality. Learning to accept change and surprises, being able to play with ideas and different possibilities, recognising the positive aspects of new ideas and challenges all help children to continue and expand the creative thinking they were born with.

Confidence in open ended situations and with open ended resources is a key factor in the development of creativity and imagination.

The environment for learning, the role of the adult, home circumstances and personal development are all key factors in children's ability to seek and organise information, think creatively, make mistakes, solve problems and evaluate their achievements.

Case study - Creative thinking

Danielle is six and a half. She is making a gift box for a present she has made for her new baby sister.

She knows that the materials, equipment and tools in the creative area are available to her at any time. She has had plenty of practice in using scissors, glue and other tools, and the wide range of recycled and other resources she can access increase her ability to be creative in her planning, thinking and making. New resources are added frequently, so there is always something new to stimulate ideas.

Danielle sits for a time, picking up and looking at the resources before starting. She collects some of the things she thinks she might use, tries these out in various combinations, and refers to the adult who is sitting nearby for advice and opinion, as she rehearses her construction.

As she works, she also thinks aloud about what she is doing, planning next stages, commenting on the textures and colours of the materials, and asking for the comments and occasional assistance of the adult who is with her.

The completed box was showed with pride to the rest of the class, when Danielle gave an animated account of her work, the problems she had making the handle stick on, and the selection of green decorations she chose because 'It's my baby's favourite colour.'

Children need access to a wide range of materials and equipment for creating their own artefacts and constructions. This will stimulate thinking, pose problems and offer variety in their learning. Children also need the confidence to use tools and equipment, such as scissors, staplers, hole punches, different glues etc. so they can work independently.

Adults need to add new resources and keep the area fresh and well organised, so new ideas can emerge and new resources can spark creativity.

The role of the adult in sustaining thinking

Adults play a crucial role in enabling children to develop thinking skills. Adults working with babies and young children need to teach, explain, demonstrate, model, scaffold and support, helping chidlren to develop the skills of thinkers. Most importantly adults should:

- give children time and space to experiment with knowledge and skills they already have;
- help them to discover things for themselves, and see mistakes as part of learning;
- support them in recognising and incorporating new knowledge;
- work with them to test theories and make propositions and hypotheses;
- provide the resources needed to support independent learning;
- offer sensitive support as children extend and sustain their thinking;
- ensure that children have models of thinkers and independent learners;
- use the language and vocabulary of thinking;
- listen carefully and patiently to children's thoughts as they struggle for meaning and sense;
- ask open questions and accept innovative answers;
- give praise and value to children's efforts, suggestions, trials, false starts and successes;

- guide them through the process of thinking about thinking, thus sustaining and extending their ability to concentrate and persevere, even when things go wrong;
- model resilience, thoughtfulness and willingness to listen to the ideas and opinions of others, to make mistakes and learn from them, to continue to be a creative adult who enjoys learning something new.

This is not easy, but it is very rewarding, and no-one ever said teaching and learning were easy!

Our Attitudes to Thinking and Learning

The previous chapters have clarified and explained how important thinking is for children's development. We now focus on the role of the adult, because children will not develop these skills unless we, as adults, have positive attitudes and commitment to proving opportunities for thinking.

- As adults we need to recognise that <u>we</u> have not stopped learning and can learn effectively alongside young children, especially if we place the emphasis on the learning experience rather than a pre-determined outcome.

- Young children need to experience thinking adults - adults who are prepared to think creatively, to take risks, to make mistakes and to learn from the children they are working with.

- Adults need to have a good understanding of child development and a positive attitude, so they can teach, explain, demonstrate, model, scaffold and support all the thinking skills children need for life.

- Having an understanding of how children learn most effectively and enthusiastically through play will lead to a more creative approach to learning and provide more opportunities for young children to think.

- Professional development and training have a key part to play in the initial and continuing learning plans of all those who are intending to work with our youngest learners.

Working with children under seven is complex and skilful, more to do with processes and less to do with product; more about learning, less about teaching. The adults who do this vital work are often under-valued and some are paid less than they should be, but they are the people who are the most important in nurturing attitudes and dispositions to learning that will last a lifetime.

Our Personal Qualities

Pascal and Bertram in the EEL (Effective Early Learning) project identified key features of adult behaviour for promoting good quality thinking, learning and development:

- Sensitivity: The adult's ability to be aware of the children's feelings and emotional wellbeing; the ability to empathise and to acknowledge children's feelings of insecurity and to offer support and encouragement.

- Stimulation: The adult's ability to offer or introduce an activity or resource in a positive, exciting and stimulating way. This includes the ability to offer extra information or join in with play in a way that extends thinking or communication.

- Autonomy: The adult's ability to give the children the freedom to experiment; support children with their decisions and judgements; encourage the expression of ideas; involve children in rule making for every ones safety and well being.

Before you start to make changes in your approaches, be sure that everyone in your school or setting understands what these key features of adult behaviour are, and uses them at all times. Don't embark on supporting autonomy and independence if you only want children to be thinkers when you say they can. Discuss any changes as a team, and talk about the consequences as well as the benefits of encouraging thinking skills.

Of course, the overwhelming benefits for children are evident in the research and in the schools and settings all over the world where sustaining shared thinking has been tried, and this evidence has had a significant effect on the guidance given to practitioners and teachers by government departments.

Involvement in young children cannot take place unless their emotional wellbeing is addressed. Engagement is similarly dependent on the adult's professional sense of self image. Do the adults in your setting feel valued, encouraged, confident in their abilities and empowered?

Question from the EEL Project Framework for Developing Effectiveness in Early Learning Settings (1996)

The Language We Use

The links between thinking skills and language development are apparent in the chapter 'How do thinking skills develop?' and are the focus of the section 'Using Language to Encourage Thinking'.

- It is of paramount importance that adults model appropriate language with young children and encourage the development of a thinking vocabulary.

- Adults need to give children time and opportunities to use their developing linguistic skills. Their ideas need to be carefully listened to and respected so they continue to use their emerging language skills to express their ideas and thoughts.

- Adults need to be aware of the types of questions they use. Too many 'testing' closed questions can prevent thinking processes from taking place. Closed questions often reduce children's answers and their thinking to one word answers, and encourage them to rely on recall. They try to give the answer they think the adult wants rather than what they may be thinking themselves. Children are also aware that adults usually ask them questions that they, the adults, already know the answer to.

- Open questions, questions that do not have one defined answer, offer children the opportunity to explore and experiment with the words, ideas and concepts they are forming in their thinking. Such questions allow adults to have a deeper knowledge of the child's understanding and thinking skills.

- Adults who use language carefully to give constructive feedback to young children are encouraging children to think. They can encourage thinking about their methods, resources, success and problems. Focusing the child on the positive aspects of their work is important too, but this needs to be specific for the children to understand their learning. A general 'that's good' or 'lovely work' is much less helpful to a child than 'I really like the colours you have chosen for the sea', or 'The way you used your hands to catch the ball was good' helps the child to learn about what they did well and what they can think about for next time.

'Why do you keep asking me questions when you already know the answers?' **Sonnyboy in:**

Listening to Four Year Olds; Jacqui Cousins; National Early Years Network (1999)

> Engaging children in planning and reflection makes them more than good actors following prescribed roles. It turns them into artists and scientists who make things happen and create meaning for themselves and other.
>
> Ann S. Epstein (2003)

The Time We Give

- Adults need to provide time for children to learn. The society we live in is very fast moving, but we must ensure that children have the time to think about and consolidate their learning.

- Adults need to ensure that there is time for children to plan and reflect, to develop ideas and have genuine problems to solve, not just answering questions posed by adult.

- Adults need to build in time for independent and reflective learning, where children stop and think about what they are going to do, have a go, talk about what has happened and then decide if they will try something different.

- Adults need to take time to listen. It is through listening to young children that we can truly understand what they are learning and thinking and thus provide opportunities for the thinking and learning to develop.

The Space We Make

- The basic human needs of comfort and safety must be addressed before the brain and body are ready to embark on learning. Adults need to create an environment where the children feel secure enough to take risks and experiment, where children know they are free to try things out, make mistakes and try again.

- Adults need to create an environment for children to think and learn. The space needs to be secure and safe, yet challenging, clearly organised and catering for all children's needs.

- Adults should be sensitive to children's learning needs, and encourage the children to discuss or change the spaces as their thinking and learning develops and matures and they begin to recognise their own needs.

Nurturing thinking by nurturing the child

Children need to feel safe and comfortable before they can develop their thinking skills. They need to feel comfortable enough to experiment, to be creative in their play and to be relaxed enough to have fun. Remember, there is a lot of laughter in a nurturing atmosphere.

Maslow's hierarchy of human need is very appropriate in our discuss of the importance of a high quality learning environment where children can develop thinking skills. You can also use it to reflect on the ethos of the environment in your setting or school.

Self-
actualisation

Self-esteem needs
recognition and status

Social needs
love and sense of belonging

Safety needs
security and protection

Physiological needs
hunger and thirst

Physiological needs

The **first and overwhelming human needs** are basic physiological needs such as **food, drink, fresh air and rest**. If needs are not met at this level, we cannot move to the next.

Children need access to water at all times, and many settings now have jugs of water and named cups, named water bottles or a small water cooler in each room. Children are encouraged to think about the need for water, and to access it frequently. Healthy snacks, available through a snack bar or at specific times, also ensure that thinking levels remain high throughout the day. Access to the garden or outside area of the setting or school will help with feelings of wellbeing and opportunities for exercise. Quiet areas where babies and children can rest when they need to can be easily provided using large cushions and draped fabrics. Fixing the fabric to the sides of the cushion with Velcro will create a nest-like area for rest or sleep that is safe enough for babies to crawl into.

Safety and Social needs

The next vital needs are for safety and a sense of belonging. If we want young children to experiment, explore and discuss, they need to feel safe and secure and feel that they belong to the community of your school or setting.

Where possible, adults should work together with children to set rules that link with everyone's rights to be heard, to talk and to have access to resources. This will establish boundaries that the whole group understand. Photos and simple positive statements such as 'We put things away', 'We listen to other people's ideas', 'We share toys and games' can help to reinforce and remind children of the agreements you have all made. If things go wrong, it is better not to ask children for an explanation; simply point the rule out to them - 'You upset James; we try to keep other people happy, have a look at the photos'. Later, when the child is feeling secure again, is the time to prompt thinking about what they could have done differently.

Clearly labelled resources also help with a sense of belonging. You can use photos or stick an example of the contents onto the outside of the storage containers for very young children, and observe babies and very young children to establish the best places for their favourite equipment and resources. Include children in setting up rules, making labels, deciding where to store resources and how to use spaces. This helps young children feel that they really belong in this learning space for the time they are in it.

Self-esteem needs

Self-esteem is the next area of need. In order to participate fully and confidently in problem solving and discussion of ideas, children need high levels of self-esteem.

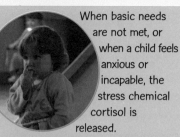

When basic needs are not met, or when a child feels anxious or incapable, the stress chemical cortisol is released. This is toxic to the brain, blocking connections and inhibiting learning.

The development of self-esteem can be supported by clearly focused praise, encouragement and the involvement of children in their own learning. Assessment for learning allows children to understand what they are trying to achieve and how they will know when they have achieved it. Children need to know that making mistakes is a valued part of the learning process, or they will feel they have failed and their self-esteem will plummet. If children are encouraged to look at their work and play, and make comments about what they like, what they found difficult, and if they would do anything differently another time, they can become more positive about trying something new.

Babies and children also need opportunities to re-visit a skill or experience, as this can reinforce positive feelings through familiarity, and is often a stimulus to apply existing knowledge to a new situation. Adults can talk about the learning and thinking that children are involved in while playing, and can ensure that the children have plenty of opportunities to revisit resources and experiences to continue their investigations.

Self-actualisation

The final and vital tier of the triangle of need is self-actualisation, knowing who you are and what you can do.

Self actualisation can be enhanced by providing physical and sensory experiences, including the use of materials which reflect images. Babies and young children are naturally fascinated by their own reflections, and at a later date by those of others they know. They need time to explore themselves and how they appear to others. Older children expand on their physical picture of themselves and begin to understand what they can achieve by having positive experiences of thinking, experimentation, exploration and research. When children reach this point, their thinking and learning develops at a greater pace, and new learning is explored for its own sake and intrinsic value.

Using Language to encourage thinking

Language is crucial in the thinking process, it helps us to categorise and name, provides meaning and connections, enables questioning and answers. Young children often talk about what they are doing as they play, and it is good to encourage this self talk, so the dialogue can continue silently as children learn to reason and hypothesise, problem solve and create solutions. Language enables children to explain what they have done or why they have tried something out, it extends thinking.

The Opportunities We Provide

- Adults should model talking for thinking. Talk out loud while problem-solving. Children need to hear how the thinking process works.

- Children need to hear vocabulary linked to thinking skills so they are able to articulate their ideas in ways that others can understand. Adults can use this vocabulary while trying to find information alongside a single child or group of children, thus sustaining their thinking. Babies and young children and babies need a language rich environment; rich in words relating to the senses, to description and discovery.

- Display relevant vocabulary in different areas of the room, or related to a project, to encourage adults and children to reinforce particular words.

- Make displays containing thinking vocabulary to encourage older children to think about the language of learning.

The role of the educator of young children is to engage actively with what most concerns the child, and to support learning through these preoccupations.

Vicky Hurst and Jenefer Joseph; Series Editors, Supporting Early Learning, Open University Press

- Tell stories sometimes, rather than reading them. Thinking about what might happen next, and using children's ideas and words in the story will encourage creative thinking and problem solving in a safe situation.

- Use puppets or soft toys and character dolls to formulate or ask questions, to model possible solutions to a problem and to ask children how they can find out about something. We are all more likely to remember something when we teach others what we know, so try to provide opportunities for children to teach each other, and to teach adults, including their parents.

- Encourage children to work with others. Whether it is exploring alongside or tackling a problem together. Working with others will extend thinking as new ideas are being introduced and discussed.

- In earlier sections we emphasised the importance of asking children open-ended questions. Questions such as 'what do you think', 'what if..?' and 'what might happen when we add ...?' open the way for thought, discussion, fact finding and more questions. Open-ended questions need to have scope for follow up, and children need to be allowed to follow the alternative ideas, to discover that there could be a better way and to be part of the process of discovery. Adults need to be encouraging and patient when guiding a child through this process.

- Paired talk, 'buddy' work and referring to another child when asked a question gives children time and space to think and rehearse their answer as they can test it on a friend. This strategy ensures that all children have the opportunity to answer and to think.

- Encourage children to ask questions - 'why?', 'how?', 'what?', 'where?', 'who?' and 'when?' are the keys to developing thinking skills. Younger children need to have questions modelled, demonstrated, supported and extended. Older children can respond to the challenge of seeing how many questions they can think of about something they have done or observed. This is an excellent way to develop their thinking, as they can then discuss how to find out the answers to the questions.

An environment that creates opportunities for thinking

Children have a right to a rich, complex environment - one that provides a wealth of sensory experiences.

Pat Brunton and Linda Thornton (2005)

Ferre Leavers, whose research and thoughts on engaging young children were incorporated into the Effective Early Learning Project (1997), puts a huge emphasis on the importance of the learning environment; the layout, use of space and the quality rather than the quantity of resources.

Think about clearly defined areas

- Areas should have a purpose so children know where to go when they want to plan, discover, answer questions, gather information, record their findings, rest or reflect etc.
- The areas may be curriculum based - writing, science, maths, art, book corner etc.
- The areas may be play based - role play, small world, creative workshop, investigation, malleable play, mark making etc.
- The areas may be experience based - as in the Reggio approach where children can express themselves, create, explore and investigate, think and reflect, be involved with others on a project, communicate, find out about themselves, find privacy.
- All areas must be given the same value by the adults and children, and everyone needs to reinforce the purpose of the areas by being seen to use each for its declared purpose.
- It is important to have relevant resources and activities to make links between each area and the outdoor environment.
- It is ideal to have a viewing area near a window or door to make a connection between the indoor space and the outdoor space.

Think about the outside space

- Outside must be seen as an extension of the room rather than a separate place to use at set times. Some children really need to be outside in order to think creatively

- The outdoor environment should reflect the indoor environment by being arranged into areas that encourage different types of thinking and learning right across the curriculum.

- There should be space to run.

- There should be space to be still and quiet.

- There should be secret spaces for reflection and talk.

- Outside is a good place to make an area for experimenting with sounds.

- If an outside area is large enough, children can have the space to think together on a large scale project or problem.

Think about high quality resources

- Resources must be of the best quality you can achieve, attractively presented and including manufactured, recycled and natural materials. If they are of good quality and interesting, children will respect and look after the environment and its resources. Using the resources responsibly will also support social and emotional skills and reflection.

- Reggio Emilio Settings in Italy look at resources carefully and try to provide 'intelligent' resources - resources that will encourage children to think, create, make decisions and problem solve. Clay, wire, natural resources, unusual and interesting recycled resources, different types of sand and gravel, ceramic and coloured glass pieces all make excellent and thought provoking resources.

- Display resources in an attractive and interesting way, so children are motivated to use or explore them. Include surprises and new items regularly.

- Display collections of similar objects, such as eggs made from stone, marble, wood, plastic, metal, of different sizes and weights, colours and patterns, all in attractive containers. These will stimulate thinking, comparison, the gathering of information and questioning. Carefully selected resources will encourage even very young children and babies to explore, using their senses and making connections in their brains.

- Resources should be stored in containers that children can access and carry safely. It is important that the children know they can move resources around the room or setting, as long as they return them to their place when they have finished with them, so that others can use them.

- Several smaller containers of a resource are much more flexible and easier for children to access and use independently.

- Babies and children need to know where to find resources so they can sustain their thinking or work through a problem or a question without having to ask an adult for help. Remember, if children can't see the things they need, they won't use them! Resources should be carefully labelled with pictures or objects to ensure easy access and return.

- Children need to have opportunities to review and discuss the storage and location of equipment and resources. They need to be involved in where things are stored, which resources go together, and how to look after them so that everyone has access when they need them.

Think about furniture

- Consider incorporating simple, everyday pieces of furniture that you would be comfortable having at home. If children feel secure in a homely environment, they will be able to think more constructively because they are less likely to have to resist the chemicals released in their brains by anxiety and stress.

- Do all the children need to sit at tables at the same time? If they do, do all the tables need to be arranged in the middle of the room? Different children need different spaces to think and learn effectively. Some need to be in a small calm space, others revel in the large social group.

- Provide child height shelving and storage, preferably without doors or curtains.

- Use pastel or light shades of colour, rather than bright primary colours which can distract rather than promote attention and concentration. If your tables and surfaces are bright then think about using fabric to change the mood of an area, display or set of resources.

Think about light

- Provide as much natural light as possible, as this encourages the brain to be more active.
- Different areas will have different light levels, and some areas of the room may be darker, so think about activities which are appropriate in more sombre and subtly lit areas.
- Add mirrored surfaces and other reflective materials to create more light in a dark space.

Think about sound

- Sound is hugely important in learning and concentration. Be aware of the acoustics of the room.
- Use fabrics and furniture to soften sound.
- Create quiet areas where sound is muffled; hang material and provide cushions to make small, quiet spaces.

Think about display

- Make a photo diary - a typical day, one child's learning journey through a chosen task, a special trip etc. This type of display encourages children to remember and make links and to talk about the learning that was happening. It also gives them ideas to try out themselves.
- Involve children in making displays of their work - involve them in the background colour paper or fabric, have speech bubbles to write their comments on, use their photos.
- Have displays that are 'works in progress', the starting point for a project, the questions the children are hoping to answer, observations of the children's problem solving and language. This type of display encourages children and adults to discuss what has happened, outcomes of decisions, and predictions of what may happen next. It gives parents an insight into how their child is learning through projects that encourage thinking, and enables the parents to ask questions at home that are relevant to what their child has been discovering.
- Display key vocabulary, either related to a topic, project or area in the room.
- Displays outside, or projected on walls are effective too, or large picture frames on walls with chalk or coloured water and paint brushes for children to express themselves.

- **Use an overhead projector or light table** to make a changeable display. Project the display onto walls, ceilings and into areas where babies are playing. Young children can be involved in making a projected display that changes throughout the day, with objects related to a current interest, project or topic. Older children can think about which objects the light will shine through, exploring the concepts of transparent, translucent and opaque. Take photos of projected pictures and display them with comments made by the children while they were working, or comments made by others when the work is finished.

- Use **interactive displays** at the children's level and involve them in creating these. You will need to think about how to make them safe, fun <u>and</u> interactive.

- **Include natural objects** in the resources available to make displays. This will increase the opportunity for children to make links with the environment.

- **Make a question board or space.** Pose questions for everyone who comes into the room to answer, such as 'What do you think the Giant in Jack and the Beanstalk would like for his birthday?', 'Someone made these footprints on our floor. Who could it be?'.

- **Put up a message board for parents, children and staff** for daily information such as 'James is going to the dentist today' and ' I am 4 today'. Of course, 'have a go' writing should be encouraged! Give children time to think about the messages and talk about relevant and important messages, giving reading and writing a purpose.

Think About Time

- **Thinking takes time!** If the activity is engaging, children will get engrossed and will almost always want to spend more time on it than you have originally planned.

- **Plan flexibly**, so you can make adjustments during the day or week for changes to plans, when children can follow up something that interests them or a new event.

- Build in plenty of observation time for adults (The NAA recommends that 80% of assessment information in the Foundation Stage should be collected during child-initiated learning). It is only through observation and careful listening that we are able to understand, support and enhance children's thinking.
- Make time to play alongside all babies and children.
- Allow time to talk with the children and discuss what they have been doing through their play. Encourage them to think about different ways they could have done something.
- Make time to stand back and look impartially at your room. Look at it from a child's eye view - what does it tell you? What can you see when you bend down to their height?

However you have set up your environment for learning you should be reviewing your provision regularly to ensure that it really does support sustained, shared thinking.

- Does my room really promote thinking?
- Does it really cater for communication, social and emotional development?
- Does it invite children to discuss, ask questions, find their own learning journey, share their discoveries in different ways to different audiences, does it give learning a purpose?

'Effective pedagogy includes interactions traditionally associated with the term "teaching", the provision of instructive learning environments and "sustained shared thinking" to extend children's learning.'
The Effective Provision of Pre-School Education (EPPE)

Thinking skills in Child-initiated Learning

If children are to develop their thinking skills they need to be motivated to persevere even when things are not going as they hoped. They need to be motivated to listen to others and to put time and effort into their play. In other words they need to want to spend time thinking.

We are born motivated, we have an innate need to find out more about ourselves and the place we are in. Babies need different sensory experiences to continue to be motivated; toddlers need real choices and some element of control over their play; young children need to understand the importance of what they are learning; and older children need to be setting their own learning goals and enjoying the achievement of them.

Child-initiated learning creates the right motivation and opportunity for developing thinking skills. In different situations this type of learning is given different names - play, choice, explore time or plan, do, review. Whatever it is called it must contain the same elements:

- Time - children need time to think, plan and investigate);
- Choice - this should be as free and wide as possible, with as little adult restriction as possible;
- Value - valued by all as an important part of the day, and valued by adults who are present with the children to support and observe their play, not trying to do directed work at the same time;
- Thinking about what is going to happen - planning of the work and activities by children;
- Supported play - where adults and children work together in sustained shared thinking
- Thinking about what has happened - review and evaluation time.

When children have opportunities to play with ideas in different situations and with a variety of resources, they discover connections and come to new and better understanding and ways of doing things. Adult support in this process enhances their ability to think critically and ask questions.

Principles of the Early Years Foundation Stage (2007)

Children need time to become engrossed, work in depth and complete activities of their own choosing.

Principles of the Foundation Stage Curriculum

Think about how to ensure that babies and young children have real choices, and chances to initiate their own learning.

Time

- Babies and young children need time to get really absorbed in what they are doing.
- The younger the child, the more time they need for their own initiated learning.
- Older children will require group learning situations and introductions to new ideas and concepts, but all children (and adults) think more about their learning when it is self-chosen.
- Children need time to make mistakes and try alternative methods.
- Children need time to return to the same activity on the same day or consecutive days. Opportunities to return to the same play allows children to try out new ideas that have been discussed or have occurred to them. Provide some space for unfinished projects.

Choice

- Provide a variety of equipment. Do you offer truly unrestricted choice of materials and equipment?
- Babies will need choice within a space or activity. If you observe them carefully you will see whether they are interested in what you have provided or not.
- As children become older they can cope with a wider range of choices.
- Children need to be able to make decisions about where their chosen activity will take place.
- Observe babies and children to ensure they are comfortable with the space where they have been placed in or have chosen.
- Observe babies with other babies and children to ensure that they are comfortable and not stressed.

Warm, trusting relationships with knowledgeable adults support children's learning more effectively than any amount of resources.

Principles of the Early Years Foundation Stage (2007)

Value

- Adults need to show they value child initiated time. They should play alongside and with children, taking part in their chosen activity. The session should be protected, and children should not be expected to undertake adult directed tasks during this time.

- For adults it is the time of day when they are able to get to know the children best. They will be able to learn so much about the children's development and thinking skills through sensitive observation, questioning and participation.

Anticipation, planning and thinking about what is going to happen

- Babies and young children need time to plan and think about their play. Adults need to give time to talking about the decisions and choices babies and children make. Even if children move quickly on from their first choice of activity, the making and verbalising of a conscious choice, rather than a random wandering among resources, is very important.

- Working in this way helps children (even very young ones) to make a decision, look at what is available, focus their attention and verbalise the choice they make. All these activities, given time and support, will expand children's abilities to think for themselves, make conscious choices and become more involved in the play that comes from them.

- Adults can support children's planning by echoing the child's verbalisations and gestures and by posing questions and provocations for the child to follow up if they wish. This will help them to get started. 'You have chosen to explore the eggs, I wonder what you will find.' 'The Lego. That's a good choice, what are you going to make?' 'You were in the house yesterday, what did you play yesterday? are you going to be someone different today?' Time spent in this reflective shared thinking will not be wasted.

In play, children's concentration and application to the task are much greater than in academically-directed activities contrived by the teacher.

Vygotsky (Palmer, S and Dolya, G, 2004)

- As children become more familiar with making choices they can be encouraged to point to the area they are going to and to put their photo or name on a picture of the area or the equipment they want to play with. Visual planners can be developed into more extensive plans of the choices they have made. However, some young children find complex recording frustrating when they are ready to start on their chosen activity. Watch them carefully and adapt the process to fit the age and maturity of the children you are working with. Offer help with recording if you think this will ease the process.

Support during child initiated sessions

Adults MUST be present during child-initiated learning. It is vital to be present so you can:

- observe and listen carefully to what the children are doing;
- play a role in the children's game as long as you do not attempt to dominate the play;
- play alongside, in parallel with children, talking about what you are doing, and why, is a valuable way to extend their thinking;
- demonstrate the use of relevant vocabulary;
- ask open questions to stimulate further thinking;
- support and guide thinking through a problem;
- help children to handle social and emotional conflicts and exchanges;
- model thinking skills by thinking aloud, posing questions, offering alternatives, using 'What if?' 'I wonder' 'How do you think...?' 'Could we...?' 'Can you think of another way?' 'What could we use?' 'How did you do that?'

Thinking about what has happened, evaluating, reflecting on play

- **Make time for this activity**. Giving children time to reflect, talk about and think about what they have been doing is very important. Remind them when they start their play that you will be talking about it later - this will help with memory and thinking.

- **Babies and very young children need this activity too**. They will need an adult to comment and look at what they have been doing, even when this doesn't have a tangible outcome. remember that taking photos or making short recordings (perhaps with a dictaphone) will help children to remember what they have been doing.

- As children become more familiar with talking about what they have done , encourage them to **sit in small groups and think about something specific**, prompting with comments and open questions such as 'Did anyone have a problem? What did you do?', 'What worked best?' 'Who did you work with?' 'Did you finish what you were making or doing, or do you want to do some more later?' 'Any ideas about what you will do next?'

- When the children are **in a bigger group**, have a system to help decide which child will be contributing this time. This will help you to manage time and **ensure all children have a chance to contribute** over time, rather than trying to include every child every time, resulting in unacceptably long sessions

- However, you need to **involve all the children** even if they are not being asked specifically. Ask them to talk to a friend about what they have been doing or be a buddy by listening to their friend talking about what they have been doing.

In play, the child is always behaving above his usual everyday behaviour: in play he is, as it were, a head above himself.

Vygotsky (Palmer, S and Dolya, G. 2004)

Part Two: Initiating Investigations and Challenges to Stimulate Thinking

Preparing the ground and standing back

Adult initiated challenges and provocations are useful as starting points for some children and in some situations. However, it is very tempting to use these as a formal programme, setting challenge after challenge, sometimes with very clear ideas about what you want children to achieve, thus stifling children's own natural exploration and investigation. Adult initiated challenges are <u>not</u> better than the ones children get involved in independently!

Here are some tips for managing the balance:

- **Observe all the children frequently and carefully**. Ask yourself if they are doing their own thinking, setting their own challenges and solving their own problems in the company of sensitive adults. If this is the case, be cautious about imposing challenges and provocations of your own.

- If you do decide to pose some adult initiated challenges, **make these as open as possible**. Don't decide on the outcomes you want. Let the children explore and follow your initial thoughts freely, coming to their own conclusions and following their own leads.

- **Maintain plenty of child-initiated time** for their own challenges. If you don't, children will lose their thinking skills and independence and will rely on you to tell them what to do.

...children make predictions, they do experiments, they try to explain what they see, and they formulate new theories based on what they already know.

Gopnik, Meltzoff and Kuhl (1999)

Some more tips for managing investigations and challenges

- Babies and children need space and freedom to develop at their own rate. Children of the same age do not necessarily develop at the same rate or need the same challenges. Expecting children of the same age to achieve the same goals at the same time or in the same way may set children up for frustration or failure.

- Challenges and investigations should give children control over their own learning. They can take on the challenge at whatever developmental level they are working at.

- Young children may be more likely to achieve a challenge alone, older children can be encouraged to share a challenge with others, as this increases the discussion. Watch carefully to see how individual children work best, and use this information to help you support individuals and extend their abilities to work in pairs or groups as they mature.

- Challenges don't have to be complicated! Changing the location, combining different resources, adding a simple new resource or thinking about something in a new way will often be sufficient to spark new thinking.

- Children need to explore and investigate what is of interest to them, so the challenges you prepare need to arise from the children's interests and projects.

- Children need the chance to be the first one to discover something new - that yellow and blue makes green, tadpoles turn into frogs or heavy things sink. These discoveries are so highly motivating that they are remembered easily because the emotional state of success and achievement reinforces connections in the brain. Stronger connections mean more extended thinking can occur.

- Motivation fuels learning and thinking. Challenges should be enjoyable, manageable and meaningful. This will encourage children to become responsible for the choices they make.
- Never forget that if these challenges are going to make a contribution to children's lives and learning, they need time to explore, experiment, discover, collect ideas, process information and come to decisions and conclusions in their own time and for themselves.

Start simple!

The investigations of babies and toddlers are about learning through their senses, making sense of the world, giving meaning to objects, making connections, beginning to give names to objects, and noticing similarities and differences. Adults need to enjoy exploring alongside babies and young children, talking about the sensory experience, posing questions such as 'I wonder what will happen if...' and modelling the language for thinking.

When working with babies and very young children, simply taking a familiar toy, object or resource and doing something unusual with it is enough to start thinking. Putting it somewhere unexpected, hiding it, combining it with another object, pretending to make it talk or move, using it with a different tool, exploring it in a different place, can all begin a discussion about differences, problems, features, feelings.

A toy car in the water tray, a drape over an empty box, a cushion and book in the garden, some bubbles, a treasure basket, a teddy in a bush, a hat worn by an adult, a new hairstyle, cooked black pasta, are all examples of the ways practitioners begin the thinking process by exploration with babies and younger children.

Sustained shared thinking involves the adult being aware of the children's interests and understandings and the adult and children working together to develop an idea or skill.

Early Years Foundation Stage (2007)

You could also offer children of all ages in your setting or school the following stimuli as standard resources to stimulate thinking:

- Sheets, blankets, light drapes, with clips and pegs, large boxes, canes, sticks and other materials which allow children to invent and construct their own play environment.

- Collections of objects to explore and choose from - bowls made from different materials, different sizes, colours and shapes, brushes, spoons, sieves and ladles, bottles and cups.

- A variety of everyday materials such as water, compost, sand, rice and jelly with spoons and other tools.

- Natural objects to explore, such as a pile of autumn leaves, a piece of turf, some gravel, shells and stones, nuts and seeds, either outdoors or inside.

- Treasure boxes and baskets, and other heuristic play materials such as lids, corks, pegs, tins, boxes.

- Sensory experiences. Sounds, tastes, textures, smells and sights to stimulate all the senses, such as 'smelly' socks in a basket - each one with an essence sprinkled on, or a collection of fabrics, paper, everyday objects that make sounds when shaken, scrunched or tapped.

- Snack time offering many different textures, smells, colours or tastes.

- Electronic toys which react to noise or vibration or a button.

As children mature and thinking skills develop, they will use these resources in different ways, with more talk and more inventiveness.

It is important to give learners the time and opportunity to talk about thinking processes, to make their own thought processes more explicit, to reflect on their strategies and thus gain more self-control.

Carol McGuiness, Brief for From Thinking Skills to Thinking Classrooms, (1999)

A rich and varied environment supports children's learning and development. It gives them the confidence to explore and learn in secure and safe, yet challenging, indoor and outdoor spaces.

Early Years Foundation stage (2007)

As children become more used to creating their own learning environments and challenges, they will be able to play for long periods of time, using adults as an additional resource to refer to as they explore, build, construct, hypothesise, reflect and refine their play, using resources and language to support their thinking. This progression will be supported by the addition of:

- **More challenging materials** for construction and building - guttering, tubes, tyres, crates, wheels, planks and wooden boxes.
- **A wider range of equipment** for exploring sand and water, smaller containers, pipettes, syringes, tubing etc as well as access to small world toys for story making and telling.
- **A mark making or graphics area** where they can use scissors, tape, staplers, pens etc to add labels, notices and signs to their work.
- **Extensions to the role play areas**, which have flexibility to incorporate children's own ideas about characters and stories, and additional materials for props, costumes and settings.
- Providing **props, music and other resources for dance and music**, and valuing these as highly as drawing and writing.
- **Places where children can reflect and think quietly**, revisiting experiences, talking with others and observing their friends at play.

Investigations and Challenges for Babies and Young Children

The activities here encourage exploration, using the senses, encouraging choice, and beginning to explore problem solving alongside a supportive adult. The most important feature is that the adult plays alongside the baby or young child, exploring and talking about what the child is doing and about their own thinking.

IT'S ME!

RESOURCES

a variety of mirrors
- large
- small
- handheld
- convex
- concave
- bendable

a variety of fabrics
- different sizes
- different transparencies
- different colours
- different patterns
- different textures

VOCABULARY

hidden	who
gone	where
find	when
seek	small
see	big
look	same
peek	different

SUSTAINING THE THINKING

- Set out the mirrors in a space - indoors or outdoors. Cover some of them completely and some partially with the different fabrics.
- Allow the children to explore and find themselves hidden behind the material.
- Explore the materials and mirrors with them.
- Hide yourself in the materials and peek out at the mirrors.
- Play peep-bo with the children.
- Exclaim and be excited when you 'find' yourself in a mirror
- Talk about what you are finding out, such as, 'I think I will see my face in this mirror. Oh yes I can see my face.'
- Ask yourself questions such as, ' Who is in this mirror? It's me,'
- Use and model the vocabulary throughout.

SOUNDSCAPE

RESOURCES

large cardboard boxes

a variety of noise making items

- bells
- crinkly paper
- crinkly material
- shakers -sealed containers with assorted objects inside such as sand, rice, pasta etc

- rattles
- toys with sounds inside
- squeakers
- music buttons
- musical instruments
- keys, beads, buttons
- little battery lights

Some children may need encouragement to go in the box at first. Take your time.

VOCABULARY

loud

quiet

ring

buzz

rattle

squeak

beep

crackle

tinkle

shake

SUSTAINING THE THINKING

- Make a tunnel from the boxes. Make it large enough for the children (and you!) to crawl through.
- Fix the different sound makers along the tunnel - on the floor, sides and hanging from the ceiling.
- Encourage the children to explore the tunnel and comment on their discoveries.
- Give them all the time they need to explore and discover all the sounds.
- Go in alongside the children and comment on the sounds.
- Encourage them to touch and squeeze the fabrics, papers and toys.
- Talk about the sounds they like and allow them to re-explore.
- Re-explore with them. Choose favourite sounds together. Try to find a sound that a bee might make, the wind, a river etc.
- Watch carefully and stop when they have had enough.

JUST A SPOONFUL

RESOURCES

a variety of spoons
- wooden
- metal
- plastic
- spoons with holes
- different colours
- different shapes & sizes

a large container
- paint tray
- sand tray
- bowl
- paddling pool

some small containers
- bowls
- baskets
- pots
- small sieves

Flour
- white
- wholemeal

(ask your local shop for out of date bags of flour)

VOCABULARY

wood	hard
metal	more
plastic	less
shiny	small
smooth	large
rough	big
reflect	round
scoop	curved
fill	full
pour	empty
spill	same
soft	different

SUSTAINING THE THINKING

- Put the flour in a large container. Set out the spoons by the flour.
- Allow the children to explore the flour and experiment with the spoons, then add some small containers.
- Play and explore with them. Talk about the spoons and containers and what you are finding out.
- Look at and talk about what the children are doing. Try to use observational talk rather than asking questions.
- Any questions need to be open ended such as 'I wonder which spoon will scoop up most flour?' or 'What do you think might happen if we use this one with holes in?'
- Use the vocabulary - children need to hear and experience vocabulary in different contexts.

ROLLING AROUND

RESOURCES

objects that roll
- variety of ball types
- variety of ball sizes
- egg shapes
- smooth stones
- lemons, oranges

- variety of cylindrical objects
- rubber
- plastic
- wooden
- metal

a variety of tubes
- different lengths
- different width
- bendable tubing
- transparent and coloured tubes

- guttering
- card tubes

bowl or box
- bowls
- thick card
- thin wood

VOCABULARY

move	when
fast	what
slow	why
roll	soft
large	smooth
medium	round
small	curved
colours	bendy
where	

SUSTAINING THE THINKING

- Start with a few of the above resources and add more if their interest is sustained as the day(s) or week(s) progress.
- Leave the objects in a bowl or box next to some of the containers.
- Encourage the children to explore and play with them.
- Play alongside, experimenting and talking about your thinking. For example, 'This tube is bigger so the big red ball might fit in here...' 'This one got stuck, I wonder why.'
- Discuss what the children are finding out and encourage them to think and talk about why the objects are moving in a particular way.
- Play hide and seek with the objects in the tubes. Encourage them to anticipate when and where the object will appear.
- Have races with different objects to see which is faster
- Allow the children to have time to re-explore, to do the same action over and over again. Offer the activity indoors and outside.
- Observe closely, comment on their actions and extending their play, learning and thinking.

PEBBLES, SHELLS AND GEMS

RESOURCES

a variety of pebbles, shells and gems
- different sizes (not too small, as some children may put them in their mouths)
- different colours
- different shapes
- varnished and unvarnished

large containers
- baskets
- wooden trays
- wooden boxes

VOCABULARY

colours	heavy
swirl	light
spiral	cool
hard	warm
prickly	pebble
shiny	gem
smooth	jewel
rough	shell

SUSTAINING THE THINKING

- Put the pebbles, shells and gems in a container.
- Explain that shells can break easily and demonstrate gentle handling.
- Put the container on a large rug or piece of fabric.
- Give the children plenty of time to explore and investigate the objects using all their senses.
- Explore alongside them. Talk about and describe what you are looking at and feeling.
- Use imaginative language - talk about what the patterns and marks look like, for example 'Look, this pebble has a smile.'
- Ask them to swap items with you. Do they think it is fair to trade a small shiny gem for a large brown pebble?
- Observe, mirror and extend the children's exploration in activities such as - making patterns, shapes, pictures, lines with the resources
  - sorting the resources by colour, shape, weight etc.

RESOURCES

real working devices such as:

- a Talking Tin (see page 88)
- electric screwdriver
- tape recorder
- programmable toy
- microphone
- camera
- telephone
- mobile phone
- torch
- computer keyboard
- CD player
- dictaphone

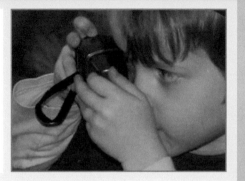

VOCABULARY

what
when
how
look
press
hold
button
light
sound
smell
work
on
off
hot
cold

SUSTAINING THE THINKING

- Ensure that all devices are in good working order, PAT tested and that batteries, if relevant, are charged.
- Put them in a suitable area indoors or outside.
- Encourage the children to explore and play with the devices.
- Stay close and observe the delight when a pressed button or turned dial makes something happen.
- Share the wonder, surprise and pleasure. Talk about what has happened.
- Encourage the child to show you what they did to make the machine jump into action - the first time may have been an accident. They may need help to find out how and why the device flashed, beeped etc.
- Ask 'I wonder what will happen if ...?'
- Talk about what each device is for and whether it is like the one they have at home or have seen before.
- Encourage the feeling of discovery and 'I can make it work', keep experimenting and talking.

<u>Never</u> leave children alone with electrical items, unless they are specially made for use by young children.

Investigations and Challenges for older children

These activities encourage children to explore using all their senses, using choice, playing with early problem solving. Adults need to talk about their own thinking and use stimulating questions to extend children's thinking.

INVESTIGATE AND SEPARATE

RESOURCES

a variety of trays and containers,
a variety of small objects to be separated:
- plenty of flour
- lentils
- rice and pasta

- dried beans
- coffee beans
- beads
- pebbles
- gems

tools for moving and separating
- spoons
- sieves
- forks
- tongs
- tweezers
- bowls
- funnels
- jugs

SUSTAINING THE THINKING

Experiment
Explore
Record

- Put the flour in a variety of trays and containers.
- Hide the different objects in the flour so that they can not be seen. Some containers may have only one type hidden inside them, others more.
- Put the tools on a tray near the containers.
- Allow plenty of free time and encourage exploration by asking open questions. Use the investigation questions here to start you off.
- Make a display with the children to record the exploring and thinking they have been doing.

INVESTIGATION QUESTIONS

- What can you see?
- What can you feel?
- How can you get the objects out of the flour?
- Which tool is best for which item? Why?
- Can you hide the flour in the pasta so we can't see it at all?
- How do tongs work?

REFLECTIONS

RESOURCES

a variety of reflective materials
- large mirrors
- small mirrors
- bendable mirrors
- convex mirrors
- concave mirrors
- windows
- shiny card
- metal spoons
- metal bowls

- black shiny plates
- plastic in picture frames
- clear plastic cups
- TV/computer screens (when off)
- glass beads
- bells
- water

a variety of drawing equipment
- different sizes and types of paper
- charcoal
- pencils of different hardnesses
- coloured pencils
- crayons
- felt pens

SUSTAINING THE THINKING

Experiment Explore Record

- Lay out a selection of resources for the children to explore.
- Give the children plenty of time to explore the mirrors without adult intervention.
- Play alongside, following the children and talking about what you are doing.
- Explore the mark making materials with the mirrors.

RECORDING

- Encourage the children to take plenty of photos.
- Offer the children a variety of drawing equipment to experiment with when drawing the way their faces and other objects appear in the reflective surfaces.

INVESTIGATION QUESTIONS

- What happens when you look in here?
- Can you make a funny face?
- Can you make one bead look like 2 beads, or 4, or 8?
- Can you draw what your face looks like in the jug? In the spoon? In the bowl?
- How many bells can you make using 2 or 3 mirrors?
- What happens if we put a mirror on the floor?

WHISK UP BUBBLES

RESOURCES

a variety of transparent containers

- jars
- food storage boxes
- bowls
- jugs

bubble mixture

- different colours
- different smells
  (buy allergy free versions to protect sensitive skin)

bubble blowers

a variety of whisking implements

- metal whisks
- plastic whisks
- metal forks
- plastic forks
- different sizes
- chop sticks

SUSTAINING THE THINKING

- Put all the resources out for the children to experiment with.
- Encourage them to use different combinations of containers, quantities of water, types of bubble mixture, types of whisk and whisking methods.

Experiment Explore Record

INVESTIGATION QUESTIONS

- How can you use the whisks?
- Are they all the same?
- What happens when you use the smallest whisk?
- Which container is best for which whisk?
- Which makes the best bubbles? Largest bubbles? Most bubbles?
- Can you blow a big bubble?
- Can you make a bubble glove?
- How can you make bubbles move?
- What's inside a bubble?
- Why do you think bubbles pop?

RECORDING

- a clipboard, paper and mark makers to write or draw
- a camera
- a video camera
- bubble prints
- talk into a tape recorder

MOVING WATER

RESOURCES

large container of water; smaller water containers and movers
- bowls
- buckets
- jugs
- bottles

- funnels
- watering cans
- plastic piping
- tubes
- guttering

a variety of things that float or sink
- boats
- wood
- light
- plastic balls
- plastic spoons
- pebbles/stones
- marbles, nails, coins

measuring tools
- measuring jug
- tape
- string (also useful for attaching to objects that sink)

SUSTAINING THE THINKING

- Offer plenty of time for free play with the resources.
- Use the questions to guide investigation.

Explore Investigate Record

INVESTIGATION QUESTIONS

- How can you move the boats along the water? Can you make them move without touching them?
- Can you get the water from here to here?
- Why does the water move in this tube and not in that one?
- What would happen if we made a hole in this bottle, where would the water go?
- How long will it take for all the water to get from here to here?
- Can you make the balls move faster?
- What happens if you put this here?
- How can you change the water level?

RECORDING

- Take photos of what happens and the challenges children undertake. Series of photos are good for recapping.

LIGHT DISPLAY

RESOURCES

overhead projector
a variety of
<u>translucent</u>
items
- material
- plastic
- netting
- stones
- gems
- lighting gels

a variety of
<u>opaque</u> items
- shells
- leaves
- grasses
- toys
- card
- string
- ribbon

SUSTAINING THE THINKING

- Set up the OHP to project light onto a projector screen or clear wall (at child height).

Explore Investigate Create

- Lay out the resources.
- Encourage the children to create their own pictures and constructions.
- You could suggest they make environments related to current interests or scenes from favourite story books.
- You could also provide projector pens and transparencies for the children to draw on as part of their play.

INVESTIGATION QUESTIONS

- What happens when you put two colours on top of each other?
- Can you make a pattern?
- Why can't you see the colour of some things when you put them on the projector?
- What happens if you stand in front of the projector?
- How many layers can you use before the display goes black?
- Can you find some other objects to add to the display? What works best?

SOUNDS INTERESTING

RESOURCES

a variety of everyday
objects that make
sounds

a basket or box

- objects that rattle
- tissue paper
- paper and card
- keys
- buttons
- leaves, grasses
- bowls, saucepans and wooden spoons
- plastic bottles part full of water

for recording

- paper or white boards and markers
- tape recorder or dictaphone
- camera

SUSTAINING THE THINKING

- Sit in a circle with the basket of sound making objects in the middle.
- Everyone has paper or a board and mark makers.
- Take turns to explore the sound makers and make marks suggested by each one.
- Now help the children to record the sounds they make, using the tape recorder. Play them back and discuss them.

See The Little Book of Sound Ideas, The Little Book of Music and The Little Book of Junk Music for more sound making ideas. All published by Featherstone Education.

INVESTIGATION QUESTIONS

- Which things do you think will make quiet sounds? Try and see if you were right.
- Which things do you think will make loud sounds?
- What is your favourite? Why?
- Can you find another sound the same?
- How many different ways can you make a sound with that?
- What is making the sound?
- Where have you heard a sound like that before?
- What else could we put in the sound basket?

ON THE SNAIL TRAIL

RESOURCES

snails and a tank
- soil
- stones and leaves

a variety of materials for the snails to crawl over
- translucent plastic
- pieces of slate
- wood

- table top
- large leaves
- black paper
- perspex sheets

a variety of trail making substances
- glycerine
- honey
- glue

- water
- cooking oil

for recording
- paper
- pencils
- timers

books about snails

Explore
Experiment
Investigate
Record

SUSTAINING THE THINKING

- Choose a damp day when you are likely to find plenty of snails.
- Set up your tank by putting soil and stones inside it.
- Go outside with the children and collect snails to put in your tank.
- Observe the snails in the tank.
- Handling the snails carefully, have snail races over various surfaces.
- Once the children have explored them thoroughly, using the questions as starting points

Return the snails to the place where you found them when you have finished.

INVESTIGATION QUESTIONS

- How do snails move? What helps them to move?
- Put them on a sheet of perspex so you can see the underneath. What can you see?
- How can you see them move from underneath?
- What happens when they move over slate?
- Can you find snail trails outside?
- How long will it take for the snail to move on wood? Table top? Stone? Wet stone? Plastic?
- Which is the fastest snail? Is it the biggest?
- Can you see any colours in the shells?
- Could you draw the patterns on their shells?
- How do snails eat? What do they eat?
- Make a snail trail yourself. Which substance makes the best trail? How did you do it?

Using Challenge Cards with Older Children

Challenge Cards are one way to encourage older children to develop thinking skills. Taking part in these sort of challenges will encourage them to use all the thinking skills - enquiry, information processing, reasoning, evaluation, problem solving and creative thinking.

Involve the children in deciding whether a challenge has been completed or whether more time is needed. Older children can be involved in talking about how they will know if they or someone else has completed a challenge, what it will look like, what they will have done? This involves them in assessment for learning - thinking about how they will evaluate their own play or work.

You can present challenge cards in a variety of ways. The ideas in this book are intended just to get you started. Set up a template for challenge cards on the computer or by drawing one sheet and photocopying it. You can then put together new challenges relatively quickly, and respond the challenges the children develop themselves by writing their words on the sheet.

Make the challenge cards available to children in the following ways:

- Read out one challenge to the whole group, and children who are interested can take it on.
- Keep the cards in a box or on a challenge board for children to take and try.
- Relate a card to a particular area of the room, an activity, topic or curriculum objective.
- Children who need their thinking extended can be given specific challenges related to their current interest or project. These could be developed by the children themselves.
- Use simple language, and add picture clues so children can read  them without adult help.
- Challenge cards can be part of an adult led session.
- Challenge cards can be part of a child initiated learning session.
- Children can set challenges for each other and adults, so have some blank cards available.
- Don't forget the occasional or regular challenge written on a flipchart, blackboard or whiteboard for children to attempt at home, during the weekend, in the playground.

CHALLENGE - <u>Which construction materials can you make spirals from?</u>

BEFORE THE CHALLENGE

The children will need to understand the concept of a spiral - they will need to have seen, felt, walked along spiral patterns, made spirals in malleable materials, with paint, crayons, mud etc. They may have found spirals patterns in nature - or the challenge may have come from a child noticing the spiral on a snail's shell.

Mathematical - patterns

DURING THE CHALLENGE

Discuss the problems. Encourage the children to record what is happening to the spirals when different materials are used. Is it still a spiral if it has corners?

AFTER THE CHALLENGE

Discuss what they found out. They may have taken photos, used a tape recorder, drawn or written what happened. Discuss which construction material is the easiest to use for this challenge, which is the hardest, and why.

EXTEND THE CHALLENGE

The children may like to see how small a spiral they can make, how large - a grand art attack!

Can they make a spiral that stands up?

CROSS-CURRICULAR LINKS

KUW: look at spirals in nature and art. Look at pictures from space of tornadoes, clusters of stars etc

ICT: using tape recorders and video and stills cameras for recording.

THINKING SKILLS INVOLVED

Enquiry: Asking themselves and others how they can complete the challenge. Tools and techniques they need.

Information Processing: What do they already know about spirals that can help them. What is a spiral?

Reasoning: Justifying the use of certain equipment, listening to others' ideas, making decisions based on knowledge.

Evaluation: Evaluating what they are doing and how it is working, both as they work and when they have completed the challenge.

Problem Solving: Most construction materials are straight edged, spirals are curved. How can we do it? How do you draw and cut a spiral?

Creative: The need to use construction equipment in a new way, combining equipment or thinking of a different way to join the equipment together.

> CHALLENGE
> Work with a friend to make spirals from paper and card.
> Use as many different materials as you can.
> Which work best?
> Test them and record your findings.

CHALLENGE - <u>Paint a picture without using a paintbrush</u>

Art - using a variety of tools

BEFORE THE CHALLENGE

Children need to have experienced mark making with paint on a variety of materials. They need to know where in the room they can access the materials they need, such as cotton wool, sponges, toy animals, marbles, cars, balls, sticks, leaves etc.

DURING THE CHALLENGE

Discuss with the children where they might go to find the tools they are going to try. Encourage them to try a variety of materials. Discuss why they chose a particular material or tool, and where they may have seen it being used before. Encourage the children to record what they have used and what has worked well or less well.

AFTER THE CHALLENGE

Talk about or make a list together of the different tools and materials the children have used. Make a display of the tools, materials and paintings. Annotate the display with the children's comments as they were working or during evaluation. Add some photos taken by the children during or after the challenge.

EXTEND THE CHALLENGE

Can they use other surfaces for painting? Does one tool or material suit a particular surface?

Can they make the same effect using a painting programme on the computer? Does it count as a painting if it has been done on the computer? Why?

MAKE CROSS-CURRICULAR LINKS

Science: did the materials used change after being used for painting?

Multicultural: look at cave drawings and paintings, what was used?

ICT: use of painting programmes.

THINKING SKILLS

Enquiry: What will work well and have the desired result?

Information Processing: What information do they have about painting techniques and methods that will be useful for this challenge?

Reasoning: Explaining what worked best and why.

Evaluation: Thinking about what else they could have tried or whether they should have tested methods first.

Problem Solving: What could they use and where would be a good place to do the challenge?

Creative: Thinking beyond the conventional methods of painting. Using fingers, feet, sticks, sponges etc.

> CHALLENGE
> Paint a picture without using a paintbrush.
> What did you use?
> How well did it work?
> Record your findings with a camera.

CHALLENGE - <u>Build an ants' nest with tunnels and rooms</u>

BEFORE THE CHALLENGE

Make sure the children have watched ants, found out about ants, looked at video footage of ants in their nests. They will need to understand how to find more information when they need it. The children can decide whether it is a nest for plastic ants, real ants or child size for role-play. They need access materials such as boxes, pipes, fabric, construction toys, wood, baskets, joining equipment and fabrics.

DURING THE CHALLENGE

Give sensitive support as they decide on the size and think about what they could use.
Support their play and construction with pictures, books, and guidance on information.
Encourage them to try a variety of materials and methods.
Discuss the use of different materials and tools, and what they know about how to use them.
Talk about ways they could record what they have used, as they work and after, to evaluate what has worked well or not. They could use video or still cameras, dictaphones, diagrams, plans, notes to record their findings.

Science - nature

AFTER THE CHALLENGE

Discuss what they found easy and hard to do, and why. Do they think they completed the challenge? Did they change anything? If they did the challenge again tomorrow where would they start?

EXTEND THE CHALLENGE

What could they use the ants' nest for once it has been completed? If it is role play size, can the children devise a story using the ants' nest as the set? If it is for real ants, where would they find them, how would they catch them? How would they feed them? How would they keep them in the nest?

> CHALLENGE
> Build an ants' nest with tunnels and rooms. It can be for real ants, plastic ants or children.
> Draw a labelled diagram before you start.

CROSS-CURRICULAR LINKS

KUW - finding out about minibeast and their homes. Using tools and materials.

THINKING SKILLS

Enquiry: What questions may they need to ask each other? Where do they find answers?
Information Processing: What do they already know about ants that can help them?
Reasoning: Understanding and explaining what they have done and why.
Evaluation: Does the nest really have everything an ant would need?
Problem Solving: Use of space and materials, fixing materials, using new tools and techniques.
Creative: the materials they choose to use, using their imaginations to create a fantastic ant's nest.

CHALLENGE - <u>Record some everyday sounds for others to guess</u>

BEFORE THE CHALLENGE
Make sure they can use a Dictaphone or tape recorder independently.
Help them to think about the sounds they choose. Encourage them to think about how they present the sounds as a game, and who they want to try guessing them?

DURING THE CHALLENGE
The children will need to work outside the classroom as well as indoors, so ensure there are enough adults to make this possible. Talk about a plan to record, play back, check each sound before moving on to the next one.

AFTER THE CHALLENGE
They need to present their sounds to others, who will they target as their audience? How will they know if the quiz is too difficult or too easy? How are they going to ask their audience to share their thoughts? How will they make sure the other children have time to write or draw each object that made the sound?

EXTEND THE CHALLENGE
Can they make a new game from the sounds? Can they make a sound walk so that others can follow where they have been? Can they use sounds to tell a story? How about making a sound tape of their home? Could they make a picture and sound matching game?

CROSS-CURRICULAR LINKS
Speaking and listening - essential skills throughout this challenge.
ICT - recording the sounds and playing them back.
KUW/Geography - the locations of the sounds they choose.

> **CHALLENGE**
> Record some sounds indoors and outside for other children to guess.
> Make them into a game.
> Test your game on some friends.

THINKING SKILLS
Enquiry: Which sounds will they record, who knows how to record them?
Information Processing: What do they know about sounds and the skills of their friends that will help them in this challenge?
Reasoning: Selecting and justifying their choice of the sounds for the audience they have chosen.
Evaluation: Deciding how the sounds could be clearer, harder, linked to a topic, make a better game?
Problem Solving: Recording sounds in a noisy environment. Leaving silent spaces in the recordings.
Creative: How can they make it fun for their audience, add in humour?

This book contains just a few ideas to stimulate and promote sustained shared thinking. Look at the resources in your setting, and use these with the children's interests to devise your own investigations and challenges to extend their thinking. Use your knowledge of the children to decide what types of activities and challenges will motivate them. As you learn more about the types of investigations they choose to explore you can add to and adapt the challenges you offer.

In the most effective settings practitioners support and challenge children's thinking by getting involved in the thinking process with them (EYFS 2007);

so that by the end of the Early Years Foundation Stage, children can:

- Use talk to organise, sequence and clarify thinking, ideas, feelings and events CLL/CT 7;

- Continue to be interested, motivated and excited to learn D&A 6;

- Maintain attention and concentrate D&A 8;

- Sustain involvement and persevere, particularly when trying to solve a problem or reach a satisfactory conclusion D&A 9.

Statements from the Foundation Stage Profile

Bibliography

Abbott, L and Langston, A	Birth to Three Matters: Supporting the Framework of Effective Practice	Open University Press ISBN 978-0335215409
DfES/Surestart	Curriculum Guidance for the Foundation Stage	QCA (2000)
DfES	Excellence and Enjoyment: A Strategy for Primary Schools	DfES (2003) www.standards.DfES.gov.uk DfES0377/2003
Bruce, Tina	Cultivating Creativity in Babies, Toddlers and Young Children	Hodder Arnold 0340814675
Brunton, P & Thornton, L	Understanding the Reggio Approach	David Fulton Publishers 1843122413
Call, N and Featherstone, S	The Thinking Child Resource Book	Open University Press ISBN 978-1855391611
Call, N and Featherstone, S	The Thinking Child: Brain-based learning for the foundation stage	Network Educational Press ISBN 978-1855391215
Charlesworth, Vicki	Critical Skills in the Early Years	Network Continuum 978-1855391840
Clancy, Mary-Ellen	Active Bodies, Active Brains: Building Thinking Skills Through Physical Activity	Human Kinetics 978-0736050968
Cowley, Sue	You Can Create a Thinking Classroom	Scholastic 9-780439-96554-5
De Bono, Edward	Message of the Day - (30/7/2005)	www.edwdebono.com
Dixon, A, Drummond, MJ,	Learning Without Limits	Oxford University Press 033521259X
Epstein, Ann S	How Planning and Reflection Develop Your Children's Thinking Skills	Beyond The Journal (9/2003) www.naeyc.org /btj/200309/Planning&Reflection.pdf
Fisher, Robert	Stories for Thinking	Nash Pollock 978-1898255093
Gilbert, Ian	Little Owl's Book of Thinking Skills: An Introduction to Thinking Skills	Crown House 978-1904424352
Gopnik, A, Meltzoff, A and Kuhl, P	How Babies Think: the Science of Childhood	Phoenix Press 075381417X
Haynes, Joanna	Children as Philosophers: Learning Through Enquiry and Dialogue in the Primary Classroom	Routledge ISBN 978-0415446815
Lindon, Jennie	Understanding Child Development Linking Theory and Practice	Hodder Arnold ISBN 978-0340886694
Macro, C and McFall, D	Questions and questioning: working with young children	Primary Science Review No:83 ISSN: 0269-2465 http://www.ttrb.ac.uk/ ELibrarianQuestionDetails.aspx?

Bibliography (continued)

McGuiness, C	From Thinking Skills to Thinking Classrooms	DfEE Research Report (1999) www.standards.DfES.gov.uk
Moyles, Janet	Just Playing: role and status of play in early childhood education	Oxford University Press 033509564X
Palmer, S and Dolya, G	Freedom of Thought	TES (30/07/2004) http://www.tes.co.uk/ article.aspx?storycode=398249
Pascal, C and Bertram, T	Effective Early Learning: case studies in improvement	Paul Chapman Publishing 0761972935
Richards, Elaine	Critical Thinking Card Games	Teaching Resources 978-0439665421
Riley, Jeni (ed.)	Learning in the Early Years: A guide for teachers of children 3-7	Paul Chapman Publishing 0761941061
Wallace and Adams	Developing higher order thinking skills and problem solving strategies in a co-operative learning environment	Gifted Education International Vol.5 No.3
Wallace, Belle (ed.)	Teaching Thinking Skills Across the Early Years	David Fulton Publishers 1853468428
Vass, P	Thinking Skills and the Learning of Primary History	Oxford Brookes University (2002) http://www.brookes.ac.uk/schools /education/rescon/Thinking%20Skills% 20Primary%20History.pdf

Useful websites and further reading

www.literacytrust.org.uk - website of the National Literacy Trust, includes research, resources, initiatives and links to other organisations.

www.standards.DfES.gov.uk/thinkingskills - comprehensive information on Thinking Skills, content prepared by Steve Higgins and Jennifer Miller of Newcastle University.

www.criticalskills.co.uk - Critical skills training programme for teachers in schools for all ages from nursery up.

try www.scre.ac.uk - for the Tooth Fairy - an Exercise in Critical Thinking.

www.talkingproducts.co.uk - for Talking Tins - 10 second recorders that stick on metal, or hide anywhere. They are made to help visually impaired adults to identify the contents of canned food, but children love them too!